The Courageous *and the* Proud

SAMUEL VANCE

The Courageous

and the Proud

W · W · NORTON & COMPANY · INC · *NEW YORK*

959.704
V222c

SBN 393 07444 7

FIRST EDITION

1 2 3 4 5 6 7 8 9 0

To MY SON, *Gary, a boy who will soon become a man, and who is also part of this great nation and truly a Black American.*

To MY WIFE, *Barbara, for standing beside me with both hands full of inspiration. In the late hours when my hunger became unbearable, her hands were always there. With all of my love, my darling.*

CONTENTS

INTRODUCTION

FOR SOME YEARS I have been thinking about writing a book about my people, the black Americans, to express the feelings of the Negro soldiers I knew and fought beside in Vietnam and to describe some of the more representative Negro leaders in the war. If I could write such a book, I told myself, it would say to the world: "See us. See us as men, see us as leaders of men both black and white." I wanted all America to understand how the Negro soldier feels about some things that are important to our country.

So this book is focused on the Negro in Vietnam and his ability to wage war and lead men into battle. I have tried to explain the Negro soldier in terms of his soldiering, his strength, courage, and will. It has not been easy to do. Essentially, this is an Infantry account. The voice of the soldier on the ground, speaking of how he felt about the war and the men he slept, ate, and fought with is the voice I heard most often and clearly.

Most Americans have never known how the Negro soldier feels under combat conditions. In past wars the black man was generally assigned to support troops. Today the Negro is in the front lines and in integrated units;

he is making his mark on the battlefield and is in command on many occasions, leading men of all races. The question is, how well is he doing these things?

What kind of change is going to come over this man after he comes home, a black hero from South Vietnam? How is he going to feel when he returns to his own land, where the majority of his fellow citizens are white and where some of them would just as soon see him stay in Vietnam?

The men described in these pages are real men, even though their names have often been changed. The place names have not been changed.

I have written the book largely in terms of conversations. Of course, they are not verbatim, but they accurately reflect what was said. Soldiers do not talk "for the record," and I have left out most of the less acceptable expressions that characterized much of the original dialogue—what sounds normal and natural on the battlefield doesn't necessarily sound that way in print, and what I have tried to capture is the substance, the content, of what was said, leaving it to more experienced writers to try to simulate the actual quality of soldiers' talk.

The book has many faults, and the author is aware of some of them. The reader will be aware of more, I am sure. But this is the story as I saw it, and the meaning I make out of it. Needless to say, I am fully responsible for everything in these pages. No one else has told me what to say and, in fact, only a few friends have urged me to say it at all.

William Sloane, Director of the Rutgers University

Press, a man with great perceptive editorial talents, has stood beside me during the birth of this book. Without his generosity and literary experience, *The Courageous and the Proud* would still be only a candle in the dark.

ONE

*A Leader
of Men*

THE JET took to the air above New York, carrying the men of the 2nd Battalion, 2nd Infantry. Behind us was Fort Devens, Massachusetts, our home for several months, where we had been trained and prepared for combat. Now we were bound for California and the Pacific beyond. The commercial airliner was cluttered with our combat gear, on the upholstered seats, under them, and in the carpeted aisle. We were not the plane's usual passengers; we were young men on our way to war. We had not been told so, but we knew. I sat back in the seat and relaxed while soft, unmartial music filtered through the speakers.

"My darling wife. My loving wife. My son." My words did not interfere with the music, because I spoke them to myself. Soldiers learn to do a lot of talking to themselves. The hour when I had left my family standing in the fresh morning air of Georgia came back to me. The airport had been crowded, but the plane I was to take had been delayed, and only a handful of people were left to see us aboard.

"You can't leave until you promise us both you'll return." I held my wife close, and saw the tears in her eyes.

"Barbara, I love you."

My son was holding on to my leg and now he began to cry. I picked him up. When I looked into his face I saw myself. My son, so close to both of us.

"I'm scared, honey. I'm afraid for you to leave us," Barbara said.

"Baby," I said firmly, "listen to me. You know me well enough to know that whatever comes I'll see it through, and I'll come back. And I'll be outstanding in whatever I do. I'm black, you're black, we have to be better than the average person. Wherever I'm going, I have to do the job better than anybody else."

After a minute Barbara stopped crying and put her arms firmly around my neck. Her voice was steady. "My faith and trust is you."

Behind the memory was the sound of the warm, soft music, but now a hand gripped my shoulder, and I heard another voice, one that was not soft and warm.

"Sarge—wake up, Sarge," the voice said. I looked up to see my squad's machine-gunner.

"What's going on, Gibbs?" I asked, clearing my eyes. "Something wrong?"

"No, you were just talking in your sleep. We'll be landing soon, and I thought maybe you'd like to wash up." Gibbs's white teeth shone in his dark, smooth face.

Half an hour after we landed and we were on our way to Oakland, where a large gray ship was waiting for us.

The bow of the transport rose into the sky above us. My men already had their barracks bags on their shoulders, and as I looked behind me I could see the others. They were stretched out along the pier for what seemed like a mile.

We spent the next two days and nights aboard the ship in the harbor. It seemed more like twenty days, but we all knew that one tomorrow or the next would be our last day in the United States for a long year. I'm sure, too, that some of the men wondered if it would be the last time they would ever see America.

Early on the third morning I was standing topside watching a seagull when a slap on my back interrupted my bird watching.

"Beautiful morning, huh Sarge?" the young back-slapper said.

"You might say that, Ben," I answered.

Ben was the radio operator for the platoon leader and everyone thought he was a kiss-ass soldier because he had made Specialist Fourth Class before the line soldiers—all the privates, that is. Before I could add anything to Ben's weather report, I saw Sergeant Gilbert walking toward us.

Gilbert came from a small country town in Georgia, and sometimes the two of us enjoyed getting together and talking over old times and soul food. "Is there a long line at the mess hall?" I asked him.

"No, there's no one down there. Everyone's topside today, trying to see all of the USA they can before it fades away," Gilbert said, stopping beside us. He was tall, dark, and, as always, his eyes were bloodshot.

Even early in the morning we were preoccupied with large questions. "Just how do you feel about going to war," Ben asked, his blond hair blowing in the fresh morning air. "I mean, like the way it is now?"

"Well," I said, "going off to war has become real. Now it's my turn to help the nation. It's also my turn to offer my life in its defense."

"You have to be kidding," Gilbert said.

"Like hell," I told him. "I have strong feelings about it. This is going to be the turning point for the Negro in America. In fact, when I get back I'm going to write a book about the Negro in Vietnam and try to explain to the American public just what we did there. Who knows, you might even be in my book." The ship's horn blasted before Gilbert could answer. For a moment we were grinning.

"When I was a boy all I wanted was to become a man and go off to war; I was sure this was the only way for any boy to become a man. Now I'm a soldier, and I guess I'm proud I'm the man with the sword, or the gun." Gilbert nodded. Ben kept on looking at me.

We all lined the rail of the ship as she pulled out of the harbor. There were hundreds of us, men of all races and from all walks of life. Some looked at the sky, some gazed out across the sea, but every one of those men was telling himself that someday he would return.

As the ship inched away from the dock, a Negro soldier bent over the rail, searching the crowd that had gathered to see us off. Then he spotted his girl and in a trembling voice shouted, "Goodbye! I love you, I love you."

The girl ran to the dock's edge and called back, "Don't ever stop!" The soldier shook his head and turned slowly away.

The girl was Negro, a lovely girl with short, glossy-black hair that seemed to capture the sun. She had in her all the loveliness of any American girl. She stood there until the ship was so far out that I couldn't see her any longer.

All of us knew our destination was Vietnam, but not once during our training had we been told by our officers that we'd be going there. Now there was no doubt.

Our first few days at sea were wretched but bearable. Then, after a week of misery, the men became restless. Tension grew, partly because with every sluggish day the certainty grew that this was no training mission. This trip was for real.

Our feelings, I guess, were the same as those of the men of World War II and Korea when they were on their way overseas, and this made me think about Sergeant West, an older Negro noncommissioned officer who had had his share of war. Two days earlier we had gotten to talking about his days in Korea. We were sitting below deck, and West was reading a dog-eared letter from home. I—the young, hopeful squad leader—had looked at him and said, "I've read about all that 'glory of war' stuff, but for some reason I feel I'm not going to find glory in South Vietnam. Here we are, sitting in the same ship that carried so many other men to other wars, some to victory and some to death. I can't help but wonder what's going to happen to me. Sure, I've got five years' training, but I'm still not sure I'm ready."

West looked over the top of his letter, slowly. "Well, I'll tell you. When I went to Korea as a young soldier I felt the same way. Before we got to Korea we made many mistakes in training, but no one was killed because of them. I wondered how it would be if the sergeant wasn't in the right place at the right time, or what would happen if a young lieutenant waited too long to tell the company commander he was lost. You'll find out the answers, Sergeant." Then he went back to his letter.

We learned something about the answers in the classes we had every day on the ship, some of which featured after-action reports from Vietnam. Men who had gone before us and made serious mistakes and had paid for them with their lives. Now we were being trained not to make the same mistakes, and we read those battle papers over and over. Other classes were on weapons, first aid, and the customs and habits of the Viet Cong. There was no problem about holding our attention, because not only were we learning things that it would be vital for us to know, but the classes helped to keep us from brooding too much about home and the people we loved. So did the ship's paper, which we read every day. The staff who put it out tried to keep us informed of what was going on in the rest of the world while the old war horse of a transport slowly made her way to Vietnam.

One day Gilbert and I were on our bunks in our corner of the ship talking.

"You know," Gilbert said, "when all this is over, I hope we black men can walk tall. Right now we're living a life of wonders, sometimes exciting and sometimes scary, but pretty soon we're going to have to just plain take it. There'll be others after us, but we black men got to prove to everybody. We got to be able to walk tall."

"When this is over," I said, "I *am* going to walk tall, very tall. You can bet on that." I hoped I sounded confident.

Gilbert looked at me. "Tell me, how come you're in the Army?"

I hesitated. Gilbert was asking me to explain something that was hard to put into words. "Well," I said finally, "I guess I had to find a way to change things. For myself, I mean."

"There's safer ways."

"I don't doubt it, but so far this one has worked. Let me give you the picture. I'm from a small country town in Georgia named Douglasville. Mostly it's a peaceful little town. The main highway runs through the middle of town, dividing it in half, and the railroad tracks run parallel to the highway. The majority of the Negroes in Douglasville live on the 'other' side of the tracks. It's the birthplace, the home, and the deathplace of many of our people. Most of the people there don't care too much about the outside world, only about things within their own circle. In Douglasville everyone knows everyone else and knows everybody's business."

"You sound as if you don't like your home town," Gilbert said.

"No, that isn't it. I loved my childhood days in Douglasville. I enjoyed hunting rabbits and birds, and I loved the outdoors. I was practically raised with a gun in my hand. The thing that held me down was that I didn't have a father. I didn't know what it was to have a man around the house. My mother tried to make up for it, but she couldn't, really. When I grew up I decided I didn't want to live in a divided town or in a half world forever. I enlisted in the Army." That was certainly a day to remember—April 20, 1960.

"And when you came into the Army, what? You found a home?" Gilbert laughed, but I didn't think it was funny.

"Hell no, man, I didn't find a home in the Army, but I did find a place to find myself, and I think I have. The Army has taught me to fight for what I want."

Then Gilbert asked if anyone had ever called me nigger in the Army.

"No. But if they had it wouldn't have bothered me. How about you?"

"Negative. But in training the sergeants gave me all the hell I could stand. At first I thought they were riding me because I was black. I didn't usually feel that way, but the pressure was on and at the time I thought it was too much for me. Later I found out the way they rode you was part of the training. I was a soldier in the U.S. Army, this so-called 'white-man's army,' and the training was for war. Still, after my eight weeks of basic were up I thought the agony was over. I never really expected to find myself on a ship in the middle of the Pacific on my way to Vietnam."

The distance between us and California grew. One day Gibbs and I were standing against the lee rail watching the whitecaps on the blue water and the flying fish skimming the surface.

"It won't be long now," I said, taking a deep breath.

Gibbs said nothing. His dark face was expressionless.

"You know," I went on, "I wonder if people at home ever stop to think about the fact that we go all over the world to fight wars so that there won't be any wars fought in the States?"

Gibbs spat over the rail. "Hell, no! People these days only think about themselves. The hell with that. My bitch is that most of the Negroes on this ship don't seem to have the slightest idea why they are going to Vietnam. Some of them don't even care."

For the first time I realized that Gibbs felt more deeply than most young Negro soldiers, that he really wished he could change the entire situation. His voice was low, and several times he looked around to see if anyone was listening. "Our mighty leaders talk about patriotism, which is supposed to be the foundation stone of our nation. But those leaders can't understand that there is a lot of unrest among the Negro people because of their treatment in America, and those leaders are all the time hollering about *dis*trust and *dis*loyalty. You got to be one hundred per cent loyal, and according to *their* definition. Yeah. But how am I, as a Negro, supposed to feel about going to a place where I got a good chance of not coming back—and then if I *do* get back I'm still treated like a second-class citizen?

"Some people say America isn't my homeland by right, that I have no heritage there. To hell with that kind of crap. I know I belong. I belong even more than some of those so-called 'true' Americans. I tell you, we got a heritage that's plenty American. There were Negroes in the ranks of the Union soldiers and with the rebels, too, for that matter. There were black men who died for this country before some of our white brethren even thought about coming to the land we call the home of the free. If you put your own life on the line, you got a right to all the liberty there is."

When Gibbs finished I knew he was a strong man, a man I wanted on my side. "I agree," I said, "and you can bet your life that if I live through this thing, I'm not going to let anybody claim any different. The story will be done on the record in black as well as in white."

He looked at me, and then he nodded. "Sure," he said. "Sure it will."

Gibbs was right—we Negroes *do* have an American heritage, but the past record was not enough for the future. Because of segregation and discrimination, the Negro had been sheltered for decades, and his ability, his true ability, had never been known. Now the facts would come into the open and be exposed to the American public. A journey of a thousand miles begins with a single step.

Days at sea, months—it seemed like years. Early one morning I was standing topside, enjoying the cool salty mist blowing across my face. For some reason Lieutenant

Burian was up, too, and he joined me at the rail. After a bit of small talk, he dropped quite a bombshell. He told me he was dissatisfied with Sergeant Mitchell, his platoon sergeant, and that he had already talked to my platoon leader about having me transferred to his platoon to replace Mitchell, if I'd accept. We talked about it until the chow line went down. I was worried about how Sergeant Mitchell would take it, but Burian told me not to be concerned about it, that he would handle it. He said that Mitchell was too old, was nervous and impatient, and wasn't even good with maps. Burian also said he'd heard a lot of good things about me and really wanted me for the post.

I heard nothing more from Lieutenant Burian for a few days, and then one evening as I was coming back from the mess hall I saw Sergeant Mitchell rushing toward me. When he reached me he was blowing and panting, and I could see he really hated me. It was the kind of hatred I had known for many years.

"Damn you, Vance! Damn you! Who the hell do you think you are, trying to take my platoon away from me?"

"Now hold on, Sergeant. *I* should be asking you who the hell you think *you* are? Get your story straight before you chew me out. I didn't try to take your platoon away. It was offered to me by your platoon leader, and if you have any questions, maybe you'd better talk to him. It wasn't *my* idea."

Mitchell stared at the floor for a minute, and then he jerked his head up and said, "I don't believe you. You're just like all the rest, and you're not gonna get my platoon. Not as long as I'm here to see that you don't. You, nor that platoon leader, nor the company commander, nor anybody else is going to boot me outta my job. Do you understand me, boy, do you understand?"

He just stood there smirking, waiting for me to flare up and hit him. But I just looked at him. "I feel sorry for you, Mitchell, I really do. Now I'm sure all the stories I've heard about you are true. You're not a man. You're not a leader. In fact, you don't even deserve those stripes you're wearing. As far as I'm concerned, this matter is closed, but I'll tell you this. The day Lieutenant Burian tells me that platoon is mine, I'll be right there to run it like an infantry platoon should be run. If you're in it, buddy, you better shape up or ship out."

I left him standing there. I looked back once and he was still staring at me with those cold blue eyes. Just standing there staring.

A few more days passed, and I didn't hear any more about becoming platoon sergeant. I thought maybe Burian had changed his mind, but finally I was ordered to report to the Old Man. When I reached the Captain's office, Mitchell was coming out. His eyes were red, and he had his handkerchief in his hand. He brushed past me without saying a word.

I knocked on the door. A cool voice from inside replied, "Come in, Sergeant Vance."

I saluted the Captain and stood at attention. He returned my salute and asked me to have a seat. He was a West Pointer, but you'd never have known it to look at him because he didn't wear his hair military style—it came all the way down to his ears. But that didn't make any difference; we all knew that he was a man every subordinate could respect, that he was a real leader.

The room was silent for a few seconds. Then he looked at me and said, "Sergeant, I've been approached by Lieutenant Burian from the second platoon, and he's not pleased with his platoon sergeant. As a matter of fact, neither am I. We've decided that once we reach Vietnam, you will become sergeant of Lieutenant Burian's platoon. We haven't yet found a job for Sergeant Mitchell, so he'll remain as platoon sergeant until we get there. But you're prepared for the job, and as far as I'm concerned, you're the man in my company who should have it."

"Well, sir," I said, "I'm glad you feel I'm capable of handling the responsibility. I'd be more than happy to accept. I feel that Lieutenant Burian and I can work well together, because I've worked with him several times during field-training exercises. But I am sorry for Sergeant Mitchell."

The Old Man stood up and walked around his desk and peered through the porthole. Then he turned and said, "Vance, I've been in the United States Army for quite a few years. I've had the pleasure of serving with good men, and the misfortune of serving with bad men. And I want you to know that the reason you're getting this job is that I feel that you're the man best qualified for it, and for no other reason. Now, when you accept this platoon I don't want you to go through your tour of Vietnam concerned about Sergeant Mitchell. Mitchell has had his day. He shouldn't even be on this ship—he should be out of the service or in the States someplace behind a desk doing something soft. War is no place for a man like Mitchell. He was in Korea. He served his time. So don't feel that you've denied Mitchell anything, because you haven't."

I left the Old Man's office feeling very proud. As it happened, I didn't run into Mitchell again. Maybe that was best.

It was a long trip, the longest I'd ever taken. The trans-Atlantic crossings on my way to and from my year of service in Germany weren't speedy, but they were nothing like this. Not as long and not as definitive. This could well be the one-way trip. We all knew it, but we talked about everything else, and a lot of the talk was serious. Some of us wrote letters, and some of us didn't, but we all talked away the endless hours.

Looking back, there was more in all that talk than we realized at the time. Many of us, including me, were making up our minds about a lot of things. I once heard that there aren't any atheists in foxholes, and it's true that some of us talked about religion quite a lot. In this area, as was often the case for me, I found Sergeant West to be a wise man. He know a lot about religion, Army-style at least. I remember one time I was sounding off about how our leaders—the officers—seemed to worry only about what they were wearing on their shoulders, their rank, and that only the chaplain seemed to worry about the rest of us. There was a column in the ship's paper called "The Chaplain's Corner" and most of us enjoyed it because there was meat in it, something to talk about and think about.

"The chaplain," I told Sergeant West that day, "is one guy who really cares about the rest of us."

"Some of them are great guys," he answered. "It was the same when I was on my way to Korea. The chaplain on that ship also had a column in the ship's paper. All of us read it. I can still remember the message he had in there just before we landed, and I bet a lot of the others remember it too. He said something like: Man has developed three basic ways of handling the problems which confront him day by day. First, he can attempt to run away from them. Second, he can attempt to fight or destroy them. Third, he can intelligently accept them and seek ways of overcoming them.

"This chaplain," Sergeant West continued, "also told us what Paul had written from a prison cell in Rome: 'I have learned to be content in whatever circumstances I am in. I know how to live in lowly circumstances and I know how to live in plenty. I have learned the secret, in all circumstances, of either a full meal or going hungry, of living in plenty or being in want. I have power for all things through Him who put a dynamo in me.' That chaplain told us things in a way we all could understand. I guess that's why I've remembered his words all these years."

On a ship, there is only so far you can go. Every day we all walked from side to side and from end to end, staring into the vast world of water that surrounded us, and I thought a lot as I walked, about many things, future, present, and past. Once while I was looking into the blue water, I asked the Lord to forgive me for all my sins, and all that I was about to commit. My prayer was: "Guide me, Lord, and keep me away from the serpent's pit. I will try and abide by your many rules but there are some I know I will have to break. There are some I just can't abide by because there are lives I will have to take. I will have to kill and destroy; I will have to do all of these things, but while I carry out my task, I will never forget you are the Almighty King." I'm sure many of my shipmates were thinking the same kind of thoughts and offering the same kind of prayers.

One of the reasons our trip was taking so long was that we stopped at Okinawa, but it turned out that only those who were staff sergeants or above in rank were to be allowed to go into town—the others would have to settle for a beer on board the ship. I learned about this from Gilbert and West, and although they didn't think it was fair they weren't as upset as I was. I was damned if I was going to go into town to have a good time and get laid if all the guys couldn't go.

But Gilbert and West went, and Gilbert reported to me when he got back that he'd had the greatest experience with a girl he'd ever had in his life. After West had gone off with a blonde (where a blonde came from in that part of the world nobody knew, but there she was, said Gilbert), he had met a girl named Jane who had treated him better than he'd ever been treated before. And even though she was gone when he woke up in the morning, she hadn't taken a penny and had told a cab driver to wait for him outside to bring him back to the ship. He said he'd never forget her, and I believed him.

Gilbert was still annoyed with me about not going ashore. He felt that I was just playing the role of the big leader, being noble, and that the guys in my platoon—most of them white—didn't give a damn about it one way or the other, and that they wouldn't when we got to Vietnam, either.

Well, I thought he was wrong, and I told him why. I'd heard that sometimes white privates wouldn't obey orders from Negro NCO's, but I didn't think this would happen to me. I felt my men respected me and looked up to me, whether they were white, black, or brown, because even though I was hard on them I was fair. I wanted it to stay that way, and I didn't feel it was right for me to go ashore and enjoy myself when there were others on the ship who couldn't. And I thought it *would* make a difference in my relations with my men.

I'm not sure Gilbert was convinced, but we didn't discuss it any further.

Finally, on the morning of the sixteenth day of October 1965, while the waters were quiet and calm and a fresh breeze was blowing over the empty deck, we reached the low, tree-lined shores of Vietnam.

TWO

Never Say
Die

VIETNAM was in the tropics, all right; the heat was almost thick enough to taste and the water was brassy under the relentless sun. As we scrambled into the landing craft the sweat was already trickling off us. This was going to be a hell of a country to fight in, especially in a war we had been taught had to be fought like a cat trying to catch a bird in the grass. We headed for the shore in silence.

Our battalion's advance unit had left Fort Devens three weeks earlier, and some of them were there to greet us, including our commanding officer. Our name for him was Colonel Smoke, but he was more than smoke—wherever he went he left a fire. Moreover, he was one hundred per cent Army, a man who lived for the service. A lot of us wondered how a Negro officer could be so completely dedicated to an organization that was practically entirely white at the command level, but he was.

He must have had a will of steel. All his subordinate officers were white and most of them, we suspected, were afraid of him, perhaps because they couldn't figure out what made him the man he was. He was hard and he was patriotic, and he was brave.

For a Negro commander to make it in the Army he has to be exceptionally good. Colonel Smoke was one of the few young Negro leaders commanding a six-hundred-man battalion, ninety per cent of it white. He had been awarded the Silver Star with one Oak Leaf Cluster, the Bronze Star, and the Purple Heart. He was considered to be one of the Army's fastest-rising Negro officers. The colonel had his faults, like any other man, but they were minor compared to his power and drive.

As we came ashore, the Old Man greeted us. He looked proud, standing at the front of the landing craft as we unloaded. With him was the division commander, and they walked among us shaking hands and talking to the men.

We waited for two weeks at the staging area twenty miles north of Saigon until all our equipment arrived and then went on to our base-camp site. Our camp area, around Ben Cat, approximately thirty miles north of Saigon, was to be our home for the next eleven months.

While we were at the staging area we ran small operations in and around the site so that we could adjust to the weather and terrain. On our first small operation most of us were excited, eager to get our feet wet for the first time. Some of the old-timers weren't so eager. They had been through this before in Korea.

We were walking along a small trail with full combat gear through an area the commanders knew was fairly safe. Soon we came to a small clearing, and the squad leaders began to fan their men out.

"Spread out over there—one mortar round will get you all," one of them yelled.

"Don't bunch up! What do you think this is, a birthday party?" another shouted.

We all were glad just to be able to walk around, but

the sun was so hot it made you want to quit right in your tracks. We went about three miles, and along the way we passed through another company's area. On the road, where everyone could see him, was a Viet Cong with his head blown half off, the first we had seen. Some of the men looked at the body and became sick.

I went back to one of my young privates; he was so sick he thought it was all over for him right there.

"Come on, Harriston, we have a long way to go," I said.

"When I saw that man, Sarge, with his head off . . ."

The first time I had spoken in a soft tone. Now I spoke harshly and as his squad leader.

"Harriston, pull yourself together. This is war. No one is here to play games, especially the Viet Cong. I'm going back up front. Don't let me find you back here carrying on like a child. Do you understand me?"

"Yes, Sergeant," he answered, gulping.

Some of the men didn't look at the dead man beside the road, and some, including me, just spat on what was left of him. It's difficult to explain, but when I passed the body I felt an urge to kick, touch, or spit on it. Perhaps I wanted to show my men how tough I was, I don't know. But I was aware that this episode was only the beginning of a long, hard ordeal.

On the evening of October 24 we prepared to move north on Route 13 to our new base camp. That night we didn't sleep much, thinking about the trip the next day. The small candle inside the large tent had long since burned out. We played cards until almost everyone lost his spending money, and then we turned in.

"Are you asleep, Sarge?" It was one of my men.

"No, Cliff, I'm not asleep; I've been lying here thinking about tomorrow."

Cliff, one of the ammo bearers in the squad, had only been with the unit for two months. He was a slender young soldier with sandy hair that always needed combing, and he wasn't too sure of himself.

"Do you think we'll have any trouble tomorrow, Sarge? I mean like an ambush or something?"

I thought over Cliff's question carefully because I knew my answer would be regarded as fact, and after a pause I said: "Cliff, you never know what to expect. You have to be prepared for all possibilities. We're soldiers. We've been trained for our job. Whatever that job turns out to be—then we're ready for it."

I guess my answer satisfied him because he went back to his cot. But most of us knew that a lot of men had been killed on Route 13. Almost every convoy had been ambushed along the way, so the odds weren't in our favor.

The next morning we boarded the trucks, which had sandbags piled around their sides for protection. At first things went peacefully. We traveled half the way without any problems, but just as we settled down and began to feel relaxed, it happened. There were bursts of fire from both sides of the road. We were ambushed.

An action of this kind is so sudden and sharp it can't be described like a prolonged fire fight. What happened was typical of a hundred other such skirmishes. Our first truck hit a mine and was blown half off the road. When it stopped, men scrambled for cover. The enemy was firing on us from the dark line of the jungle.

"Spread your men out, Sergeant Vance," the platoon leader yelled. "Set your machine gun up on the right of that small ridge."

My gun was in place in minutes, and Gibbs began firing all across the platoon's front. And then, for the first time since we'd arrived in Vietnam, we heard it—a cry for help.

By the time someone reached the man who had cried out it was too late. He belonged to another unit, but somehow had got in with our company.

After a brief fire fight, it was all over. We began rolling ahead again, but we were pretty quiet. We had a lot to think over.

That evening we reached Lai Khe, the site of our base camp. Our work was cut out for us for the first three days. We began building bunkers, defense positions.

"How long do you think this will last?" I asked Sergeant Marsh.

Marsh was leader of the third squad in the platoon, and he had also seen combat in Korea. My position was next to his on the platoon front. When things got rough, his favorite expression was "Let's get drunk and get naked."

"We dig all day and stay up all night, looking and waiting for the Viet Cong," he answered, scratching his behind. "This crap can go on for days. Just when we think it's going to get better it'll get worse."

"What do you mean?"

"The same thing happened in Korea. When we thought things were all right, hell broke loose. Maybe the big war there was different because it was more conventional, but the little pattern is going to be basically the same here."

Every morning at about five we started for the jungle on operations called "sweeps" to look for the Viet Cong or his hiding place. Day after day we roamed through the jungle sweating like boxers in the fourteenth round of a fifteen-round fight. If it wasn't the heat—and it was 100° all the time—it was red or black ants getting into our clothes.

We stayed out all day every day looking for the Viet Cong but never finding him. When we got back to base camp, some of us pulled guard duty all night and so got no sleep or rest that amounted to anything. Then, before the sun rose we'd make quite a few miles in the jungle.

The men began to get tired; every day was the same and we never found the Viet Cong, not even a trace of him. By now we all began to itch for some action, but the VC didn't cooperate.

Once, after a hard day of working on our positions in the base camp, some of the noncommissioned officers gathered at the platoon command post for a cold can of beer, something that didn't happen very often.

"I can't wait until I can get one of those little slope-heads in my sights," said one of the platoon sergeants, a short, fat man named Baldwin who did not belong in a line unit. In fact, the company commander had almost relieved him one time on the ship. "I'm sure I could kill one of them without even thinking twice."

"You say that now, Baldwin," Sergeant West retorted, "but when you're confronted with one of those little men maybe you'll change your way of thinking."

"Maybe so, but right now that's the way I feel."

I listened to them talk for a while and then I heard myself saying, "Nice American boys have turned into barbarians. Maybe we mean what we're saying, but I doubt it. This is one of the advantages the VC has over us—his ability to wage guerrilla war. Sleeping in holes every night full of mud and water, with the mosquitoes all over you, something's going to give."

"Has anyone heard how Sergeant Tye is doing?" Sergeant Marsh asked.

"Who's he?" said Baldwin.

If Sergeant Tye was white, I said to myself, Baldwin would know him. "Sergeant Tye is a squad leader in the second platoon who came over with the advance party," I told him. "He's about forty-one and in prime condition. Anything that comes up, the Old Man calls for Tye to do the job. He's being used like a horse. Tye's a Guamanian, next door to being a Negro as far as anyone else is concerned; he may as well be black. Tye's never complained to anyone but me, but I know how he feels because I have the same problem he has in a round-about way."

"What do you mean?" Baldwin asked.

"I mean that every time the Old Man wants a platoon

for a tough patrol, the only platoon sergeant he can think of is Sergeant Vance."

"What the hell happened to Sergeant Tye, then?"

"Well, two days ago Tye was sent to Saigon on a convoy, but he never returned to the company area. His truck hit a land mine—broken back, two broken legs, fractured skull, and loss of sight in one eye. He's disabled for life."

Weeks passed. We became accustomed to the country and some of the ways of the Viet Cong. We had small operations every day and they were all the same. Some of the men on ambush patrol in the pass to the northwest of us had made a little contact, but nothing that lasted.

One evening as I came in off patrol I found Gilbert sitting near my command post staring out across the wire we had in place in front of our lines. He sat there looking as if he didn't have a friend in the world.

"Long time no see, Gilbert. Where have you been keeping yourself?"

"I've had my hands full, so damn full, in fact, I don't know if I've been coming or going."

"What's the problem?" I said as I took off my combat gear.

Gilbert's dark face has lost its shine. "Just about every patrol that goes out from my platoon—I'm the leader. They act like I'm the only sergeant in the damn platoon."

"Me, too, Gilbert, and I was talking to Sergeant LeRoy, the Negro sergeant in the third platoon, and he was saying the same thing."

"I know, but it's not right."

"What the hell can we do about it? We've only been in the country for thirty days and they're already trying to kill us off. The first ambush patrol in this company was led by a Negro. All the Negro noncoms in the company are considered the best in the battalion and they're being used to death. Every time there's a dirty job to do, you can bet a black man will be in charge. Maybe they *are* trying to kill us off. But I know too that the Negroes in our unit are the best we've got, and so does the company commander."

"Everyone in the company knows that. The first real action the company had, the patrol was led by a Negro sergeant—Davis."

I often wondered if it was really true that Negroes were being assigned the most dangerous patrols and that they got less consideration than they deserved in the light of their performance, which was good, very good. One thing seemed clear: The men in our squads certainly didn't question us or our orders, and if the Negro noncoms were being given the roughest assignments, then the men they led, white and black, were also getting the ugly end of the stick. But their morale was good, and there was no grumbling beyond the normal and healthy amount.

In the weeks that followed, we lost a lot of men and we killed a lot of VC, but the action was not enough to satisfy most of us. We had come a long way to do a dirty job, and we felt we weren't getting it done fast enough.

We wanted more action, or else we wanted out. Every once in a while someone would get away from the jungle and the heat and the mud and the endless patrols for a time. Gibbs did when his mother died and he was flown home to her funeral.

When he returned he came into the platoon wearily with his barracks bag on his shoulder. I met him near the command post.

"It's good to have you back, Gibbs, but I'm sure you'd rather have stayed at home."

Gibbs grunted. "I don't know. Things at home aren't the same now, and as far as I'm concerned they won't ever be the same."

I was surprised. "I don't follow you. Why aren't they the same?"

"Maybe because they haven't changed and I have. On the surface there's no difference. After my mother was buried, I felt the same old hostility from the whites. But I was remembering all the fellows in Vietnam: I thought of how the black man sleeps beside the white man in the mud and rain. The black man looks upon that white man as a man, as a friend, as a soldier, but most of all as an American. When we see a man, no matter what color he is, lying on a jungle trail with his head blown half off, we feel compassion; we hurt inside. If only the people back home could feel that way about us, without looking at the color of our skin. I was wearing my uniform downtown, and people still treated me like I was dirt. That was when I wanted to get back to Vietnam."

Negroes have to be tough, I thought. Gibbs had just

lost his mother, and he had no wife or children to go to for a little comfort. So, with strength, courage, and devotion to duty he just returned to the war. It was almost as if the war was the only home he had. That didn't seem to me the perfect advertisement for my country.

Gibbs stood looking at his uniform. The letters in gold on his chest read "U.S. Army." A shot was fired from one of the nearby platoons and both of us took cover.

"Why don't you relax for a while, Gibbs?" I asked. "Try and get some sleep."

"No—no sleep right now. I'd like to talk. There's a lot I have to say."

I listened and tried to make him feel that I understood as he talked about a lot of things—problems at home, and how he felt about things there.

Then he said, "A man can be subjected to many things that test his ability, but sometimes I wonder what this ability is. A wish for survival? Survival is the basic law, and each day here it's challenged—but each day also gives us the opportunity to share."

These occasional talks, these quiet times when we tried to figure out what things were really all about were, of course, partly the result of being in constant danger. But war was our business and it took up ninety per cent of our time. We had to leave the basic questions to someone else to figure out.

Gibbs was only one of my problems. There were moments when I felt like I had more than my share, but I had to push on and always keep the enemy on my mind in the midst of this frustrating war. There were forty-three men under me, and I was responsible for leading them. Long hard day after long hard day, leading tired men in suffocating heat, I think even my own thinking became fouled up on occasions. We didn't make many contacts on our sweeps, but we had to fight the terrain and the climate every day. Hot sun, thick jungle, red ants, monsoon rains, mud up to our waists, these things picked away at us every waking moment. Our will, our determination to drive on, was sometimes sapped to the point of danger.

Fortunately, good soldiers have a certain spirit to off-set this wearing away of the combat drive. You hear it when the going gets rough: "Hang in there," they'll say, or "Keep on pushing," or "Drive on." This helped us keep going, helped us remember our mission. Still, we couldn't help but feel frustrated. We wanted to make heavy contact with the enemy, and so far we hadn't.

After I took over the platoon, I made a lot of changes and ran the unit very firmly and fairly—at least as I saw it. In doing so, I took on many titles. Some of the men called me the "Black Warrior" and some called me the "Fearless One" (which I suspect was not completely a compliment), but the name I was best known by was "Big V," since my last name began with V and I was taller than most of the others.

My friend Corporal Gibbs finally made sergeant and was about to lead his first combat patrol. As he stood in my command post I could see the pride in his face.

"Well, Gibbs, today is the day for you."

"That's right. You have any special instructions for me?"

"No, I gave them all this morning." He just stood there staring at me.

"What's wrong with you?" I asked.

"I feel very sure of myself, Sergeant Vance, and it's because of your standards."

"High standards are mile-posts on the road to victory," I replied. "Also to survival."

Gibbs took his patrol out and did a very good job.

One morning my platoon was sent out on a patrol to intercept a squad of Viet Cong who had been spotted about five hundred meters in front of our lines and who were thought to be the snipers harassing the second and third platoons every other day.

For some reason, I felt that this patrol might bring us to the hour of truth. Even though we'd never made real contact on a patrol before, I knew today would bring either victory or defeat. The jungle was unusually quiet as we cut our way through the thick undergrowth. Suddenly the point man held up his hand. We stopped and got down, and I went forward to see what was wrong.

"I can hear them walking down the trail, Sergeant," the point man said. We set up a hasty ambush and waited for the Viet Cong to enter our "kill zone."

Then, there they were, walking down the trail in their black uniforms, strutting as if the war had ended. At last we had found the enemy. I looked at my men. They were a little nervous but patient, and so was I.

Seconds later I signaled to open fire. Thunder clapped as the hand grenades exploded, lightning struck as the machine guns fired 550 rounds per minute, laying down a deadly blanket of lead. We fired all our weapons, trying desperately to destroy every last VC. They fought back but they were outclassed, outnumbered, and caught in our deadly trap.

One Viet Cong, screaming like a mad man, with blood streaming down his face, refused to die. Suddenly I realized he was the man assigned to kill the leader, and he was coming for me. He must have lost his rifle; he was charging with only a knife. I raised my automatic rifle, but before I could squeeze the trigger I felt his knife sink into my left shoulder.

We fell to the ground, he on top of me. I gave him a smashing right to the head and he fell away from me, dropping his knife. Fighting frantically for my life, I grabbed his knife and plunged it into his chest—once, twice, until he no longer moved. The firing had stopped. I looked down at the dead man and said, "Oh God, this is as close to death as I want to get, please Father, no closer, and no more."

One of my squad leaders touched my shoulder.

"Are you okay?" he asked.

"I'm okay," I answered. All of my men were alive and I thanked God for that.

One of my young privates came up to me and with tears in his eyes said, "Sergeant?"

"Yes?"

With a catch in his voice he said, "Drive on"—a little saying we had when times were rough.

THREE

The Battle of
Bau Bang

After a rest in Third Field Hospital in Saigon I returned to my unit, just in time to take part in a road-clearing operation north of Ben Cat near the small town of Bau Bang. I found my platoon preparing for action. As I looked them over, I felt a sense of pride. They looked, to a soldier, like a good fighting force. Everyone seemed glad to see me and I was glad to be back.

Sergeant Kain, my weapons' squad leader, told me about our operation order for the next day, which was to clear Route 13 and hold it for a Vietnamese unit traveling north. It sounded like all our other missions. Kain also said, however, that the men had had a chance to rest a few days before going out, which was unusual—three days in base camp was a record for us, as we'd never stayed in over two days before. He felt that we were really ready to go out again.

"It sounds like most of the men are still hot in the pants to make contact," I said.

"That's right, Sarge. We're still hungry for contact with the enemy. We're fed up with searching the jungle for something most of us have never seen."

"Okay," I said. "Maybe this time will be it."

The next morning we were on our way. The notorious Route 13 was covered with troops as far as you could see. My company had one unit of armor and one crew of support troops. The drivers of the armored personnel carriers were gunning their engines, and the other men were a little excited because this was the first time we had operated with APC's.

The first day went as planned, almost like any other operation. At night we set up a defensive position on the east side of Route 13. After we stopped for the night we were all tired, but no one complained very much.

"What do you think of this first day?" I asked Gibbs as he cleaned his machine gun.

"I don't know. It's a little unusual, but I guess it's going to be okay. How does it look to you?"

I hesitated and then decided on frankness. "I don't like this position. Too many lives have been lost on this highway, old Bloody One-Three. We don't know for sure, but some real action could be near—so near that some of us might not be around to wish for any more later."

It didn't really seem like the area we were occupying was worth defending, but when your orders are to occupy, that's what you do. You don't ask questions.

The Viet Cong had a well-planned attack set for us that second night—the VC usually had a good plan—but they thought we were going to set up in the same area the following night, so they planned their attack on our old position. That's where we were ahead of them. We moved a quarter mile and regrouped, but it was late and we had to move fast. Sergeant Marsh and I made our bunks on the back of the APC assigned to us for the operation. The weather was bad that night, but for some reason I didn't bother to dig myself a foxhole.

About an hour after dark word came down that some kids from Bau Bang were selling beer and Cokes near the entrance of the village, close to the right flank of our lines.

Some of the men bought beer from them, not knowing they were Viet Cong agents. Of course, all of us knew the Viet Cong were in the area because we had the intelligence reports that there were about a thousand VC operating around Bau Bang. On the eleventh we moved north about two thousand meters, clearing each side of the road about a hundred meters.

The advance went okay, even though during the day we got some sniper fire from the jungle lines. Two men were wounded and another killed before the day ended. We got some action, but not the kind we were expecting. The Viet Cong were using the hit and run, and we never had a chance to fire even one shot.

That night we moved south again. We passed the area we had occupied the night before and formed our positions on the west side of Route 13 just south of Bau Bang.

There had been thirteen personnel carriers in my platoon area. The first squad took the left side, the second had the center, and the third covered the right flank. Each area had one M-60 machine gun. I made my command post on the right flank with my first machine gun crew. During the early hours of the evening we all worked like hell to dig prone shelters before darkness, and I was busy putting up my hammock between two rubber trees. We all settled down to what was supposed to be our last night in the field. About five hundred meters in front of the battalion, our company had a squad-size ambush patrol that also served as a listening post for the battalion. Shanklen, a Negro sergeant in the third platoon, was the leader.

At 1700 hours Shanklen had received his patrol order from the company commander. He was to take his squad of thirteen men and move about five hundred meters south of the battalion and set the squad up for a possible ambush of VC troop units moving in our direction. After dark he started to move his patrol through our lines. The men's faces were blackened with dirt to keep from reflecting any light that would give away the position. In an hour they reached their designated site, where they found a small trail running parallel to the battalion. Shanklen had selected that area for the ambush. Even though it wasn't the best place for an ambush, there were many reasons for staying there.

Two hours later they heard a noise. Down the trail in front of them, the enemy was approaching, very slowly and cautiously. They held their fire until they could see the shadows of the VC, but then they realized it was only one man, and not worth firing at, because it would only have given away their position. Again they waited. In the morning around 0500 they heard the enemy coming again, and this time it was more than one. As soon as all of the shadows were within the killing zone, Shanklen's men opened fire on what they thought were about twenty men, and they got most of them.

Shanklen thought everything was under control, but,

without warning, it was as if every tree in the jungle had a gun and had begun firing. The fire was so heavy that he knew his squad was greatly outnumbered and about to be overrun.

Over the screaming and shouting Shanklen gave the order to pull back to the alternate position. Some of his men pulled back and some tried to help others but they were killed in the process. They fought for dear life, knowing that if they didn't, it was the end for them all. The Viet Cong rushed in, firing in all directions. With one last desperate attempt to pull back, Shanklen and his men gave them all the fire power they had.

Sergeant Shanklen called his company commander and said, "Sir, sir, we're being overrun; the Viet Cong are all over the place. I've lost most of my men. Help us!"

The only answer he received was, "Do the best you can and get in your holes."

What Shanklen really felt then nobody will ever know, but he said later he felt like shooting his company commander first and himself second. More than half his men were dead before the fight was over, most of them Puerto Rican. He wondered what the great white company commander would have done if his patrol had been all white.

After hiding out all night, watching the Viet Cong take what they wanted from the dead, four of the squad, including Shanklen, made it back the next day.

This action was the beginning of the Battle of Bau Bang. Shanklen's patrol had sprung the attack. They were the guinea pigs for the rest of the battalion and had warned the rest of us. Because of that warning, the Viet Cong were not able to launch a surprise attack.

Even after the patrol out front was hit, the rest of us were still not sure whether there was anything to get excited about. Then, at approximately 0600 hours we received word to get ready to move. Thirty minutes later we heard 60-millimeter mortar sounds coming in, and all of us scrambled for our holes. Sergeant Marsh shouted to his men to get into the APC parked beside his position, but by that time the entire action was a nightmare. Everyone was firing, men were screaming, and blood and death were all around us.

All during the night the Viet Cong had been crawling toward our position, and they had their machine guns set up only about thirty meters from us. In the early morning we heard a loud explosion: the APC the men had climbed into had been hit by a 57-millimeter recoilless rifle. A gush of smoke shot out of it, followed by fire and the smell of burnt flesh.

Sergeant Roberts, on my left, dashed over, under fire, to help the men who were still alive. With sweat rolling down his dark face, he worked desperately to free the wounded. Meanwhile, the Viet Cong were attacking us from all sides with everything they had. Clearly intended to destroy us. Their fire hit the APC's, one after the other, but our men held the line with superior fire power. Still, each time an APC was knocked out, the 50-caliber machine gun on its top was silenced, and someone else had to get up there and fire the gun.

All this time we didn't know or have any idea of the

size of the force that was attacking us. With the Viet Cong shouting and screaming, machine guns, hand grenades, you could hardly hear the man beside you. I found out it's not true that during your first battle you don't have time to think. You're thinking all the time about staying alive and about what you have to do to stay that way.

The Viet Cong kept trying to attack, even though they were taking heavy losses. My platoon was catching the brunt of the battle from the right front, but the command post in the rear was being hit hard too, and I didn't receive the orders from the Old Man that Sergeant Shanklen had. The Viet Cong had the command post zeroed in with mortars and they were knocking out all of the trucks back there.

Finally, the Air Force came on the set. They made pass after pass on the enemy positions and really clobbered them. Sometimes the planes came so close to the ground you could feel the heat from their engines. Every man in the platoon must have thanked his God for the Air Force. Without those planes we might not have made it.

When the Air Force had finished dropping their bombs and firing their rockets and 20-millimeter cannons, not many Viet Cong were left alive. Over 430 VC were dead and a great many were wounded. We lost at least six men out of my platoon alone that day, but the VC paid for them many times over.

After many long hours, the battle finally ended. The field was covered with enemy bodies, broken weapons, and all kinds of war gear. When we searched the Viet

Cong bodies, we found that some weren't more than sixteen.

When the shouting stopped, we picked up our battle gear and walked away to complete the mission we had set out to do, proud that we had beaten a force five times our size, even though we were saddened that we left behind us some very good men. As we left the battlefield and the litter of the dead Viet Cong and Americans there was bitterness in our pride. As they walked around the dead Viet Cong, some of the men stepped on their heads, some kicked their faces in, and some just looked and walked on. The American soldier can be as brutal as any man alive during war.

Then, as we came onto Route 13, there was a big explosion. Men hit the dirt and began to take cover. Three more of my men were hit, and an entire machine gun crew was wiped out.

When I got there, one of the gunners was lying in the middle of the road with his legs twisted and his ankles and feet blown completely off. It was Matterison, who had never harmed anybody, who had always helped others.

Looking at Mat lying there mutilated and looking at my other wounded men, I asked myself if all this killing was worth it, and I couldn't help thinking of the parents, the wives who would be told of the deaths the next day.

But I was proud of my people. I'd always known that black men would measure up in combat, and the Negroes in the platoon did more than their share of duty. They had paid no attention to their own safety.

We were given more time than usual before the next big operation, so we had plenty of time to talk and hear stories about the parts of the action we hadn't seen. I didn't talk too much myself, but I wanted to hear other opinions.

I got many of the men in the company to write what they thought about the battle. I asked them how it affected them personally, what they thought of the battle as a whole, and to comment on anybody they particularly noticed during the fighting.

Among the things they commented on was the fact that we were ordered into battle with insufficient intelligence reports on the number of enemy troops in the area and that therefore we hadn't taken sufficient precautions to protect ourselves. "We were sitting ducks, waiting for the hunters to arrive," was how one sergeant put it.

There was also a strong suspicion that on too many occasions the commanders would needlessly jeopardize their men's lives by sending them out against overwhelming odds just to make a good showing, to increase their own chances for promotion.

There were complaints about defective equipment that maimed and killed our own men every day, and that these things just weren't taken seriously by the command.

There was also a general feeling that morale was low because it was hard to keep morale up while fighting in a war the men knew nothing about and in which the people being helped—the South Vietnamese—weren't doing their share of the fighting. This was backed up by a feeling that the government leaders in Saigon were corrupt and were more than willing to watch the Americans doing their fighting for them.

And there was a feeling that the morale among the Negro troops was even lower because they were so aware that they were in Vietnam in the service of a country that didn't treat them—or their families or any of their people —like human beings at home.

On the positive side, there were reports that Negro leaders had performed consistently well, and that some men had proved their true worth in battle and had begun functioning with an ability and sureness they had never shown before.

But not all the men had proved themselves in battle. One who hadn't was Sergeant Lamb, who was a particular problem to me. Sergeant Lamb had lost control of himself during the battle, and although I tried to be sympathetic with him, I came close to hating him, because of the men who had lost their lives instead of their self-control—and we'd have to fight with him by our sides again and again.

But part of the responsibility of leadership was to take all my men as they came. And there was another thing: when Lamb talked to me I realized that he—a white man who I'm sure had never thought of the black man as his equal at home—needed to explain himself to me, to cover up his weakness in battle. He actually wanted understanding, not only from a fellow sergeant but from a Negro. Maybe, in spite of everything, the war was making us take one of the steps forward I'd always hoped for.

The story he told me to justify his behavior in battle

just didn't stand up, even though he wanted me to believe it and wanted to believe it himself. The rest of the company knew the truth about Lamb, knew that he was no good in combat, and stayed away from him. Even on easy patrols he got so upset that he made everyone around him nervous.

One day not too long after the Battle of Bau Bang, when we were still hashing it over and speculating about what might be coming next, I had a visit from Pfc. Allen, a young white soldier who had a good record.

In spite of all my years in the Army and of my trust in its essential integration and its disregard for all kinds of classifications except military ones, I felt troubled for a moment before talking to Allen. It was easier to talk to my Negro comrades, and we had been able to help each other a lot, because there were certain things that only we understood. But I was responsible for both the Negro men and the white men under me, and I had to try—and try hard—to understand them all. I wondered if the white officers and NCO's had this same feeling when a Negro came to them.

This doubt was not a new one. Combat command depends on the assumption that an order will be obeyed if it is from a proper source, in an almost reflex way. You salute the rank, not the man. But combat is the smallest part of the time served in the Army, and the man, not the rank, can be important. I had often wondered if there was any resentment about the number of Negroes who were commanding the details of a combat operation like Bau

Bang. Sergeant Lamb, for example, hung heavy and un-resolved in my mind—was I critical of the man, or of the fact that he was white? These and a lot of other things went through my mind while I was looking up at Allen.

"My squad leader said it was okay for me to talk to you, Sergeant Vance," Allen said.

"Sit down, Allen. What's on your mind?"

"Well," he said slowly, "I guess it's what's on every-body's mind, most of the time. The battle. You been col-lecting stuff and getting guys to talk, and even to write things down. I guess you have to know what kind of job the NCO's did, the sergeants and so on. But if you're col-lecting stuff about the battle, somebody ought to brief you about the privates."

I wanted to laugh but held it to a grin. "No argument, no sweat. I happen to know you did an outstanding job yourself, so I guess you don't want any sympathy."

"Hell, no," he said. "I just wanted to tell you that in this battle, maybe just this particular battle, some of the privates turned out better leaders than some of the ser-geants, and maybe you'd like to hear a private's version."

Allen described the fighting from his point of view, and I listened carefully.

"I was more afraid after the action, Sarge, than I was during the fight," Allen concluded. "When it was over I had time to think about what was going on. It was far from the glory it was advertised to be."

"No one's going to find any glory here in Vietnam," I said. "When we moved out we all felt real good because we knew we had won. Then that Claymore mine went off and wounded five of my men. I'm like you. I don't like to hate, but I guess you can't help it sometimes. That was when I gave the order to burn everything in our path and kill everything that was alive."

Allen sat quietly and then he said, "That was a sad day, Sarge, one I'll carry to my grave. But there are other things—good things—I'll remember too. Private Garry, for one—a really brave man, and the only medic to have around when the going gets tough. He's our morale booster, even if he is in his thirties and has been up and busted down in rank. He knows his way around."

"Have you talked to Doc much?"

"Not recently, but when he was assigned to our squad for a patrol we talked almost all night. Old Doc has a weakness. He drinks."

"Yes, that's right," I said. "Drinking has always been his problem. When we were in the base area he was always away and in trouble, but when we went to the field he was right there. Doc is white, but he was always with one of the Negro men. The people in my home town have a name for whites like him—'nigger lovers'—whatever that means."

"Doc will always be my friend; he could like the devil for all I care. I know you think a lot of Doc, too."

"When I think of men like Garry," I said, "I wonder if I'm doing the right thing—being here in Vietnam, I mean. Some say the only good Negro is a dead one, and I used to say that the good white is the one who was never born. Now it's not that way. I'm a Negro, sure enough, but also I'm a sergeant. I've got responsibility for other men's lives. I can't think the way I used to any more. All I can see now is that a man is a man."

Allen smiled. "The men in this platoon respect you. So do I. There aren't many platoon sergeants who'd talk to me the way you have. So long, and thanks."

I watched him leave, I thought to myself, there goes another white man who has some real understanding. Then I picked up my pen and pad to ~~wrote~~ to my wife, but I changed my mind. I decided instead to write to the mother of one of the white men who was killed during the battle. For some reason I felt compelled to make a point of telling her that I was a Negro and I felt that she would like to know that fact. After writing a draft of the letter, however, I wasn't sure if I was doing the right thing, so I didn't send it right away.

After thinking about that letter for a week, I sat down one evening and rewrote it.

Dear Mrs. McClure,

You don't know me, but I truly hope that when you receive this letter it will find you and all your family in the very best of health. We received the cake you sent us a few days ago, and I speak for all the men in the first platoon by saying it was the best cake we have ever tasted.

Your son was a proud member of this small unit. There isn't a man here who could say that he was anything less than a wonderful person to know and be with. I was his platoon sergeant and he was one of the best men I had. We were together most of the time. I believe he had the greatest respect for me, and I have nothing but praise for your son. Militarily speaking, also, you have every reason to be proud of him. We were together during the battle and in the face of the enemy and death. I want you to know that he handled himself like an American soldier.

I am Negro, Mrs. McClure. I think you might like to know that. To your son, I was his leader and I think that's the way he always thought of me. This is one of the reasons I can say that men like him just don't come any better.

When I didn't hear from Mrs. McClure for quite a while I began to feel that I had been correct about how whites must feel about Negroes, and that maybe she thought I wasn't worth writing to. Then I received a letter from Mrs. McClure, a letter I will always remember.

Dear Sergeant Vance,

I am glad that you were able to know my son, and I think I can feel the sincerity in your kind words about him. We saw him grow up with a strong loyalty to home, family, religion, and friends, and I always felt that when he was away he would show that same loyalty to his buddies and friends. If we are to be proud, sergeant, as you tell us, I think that what we are really proud of is his love for his fellow man and his desire to help him in any way possible. We pray that his death will not have been in vain.

Please understand that we would like to hear from you again, and we are wondering if there is

anything we might be able to send that might be enjoyed by you and your men. We feel so helpless. . . .
Don't hesitate to ask. God bless you and keep you.

After reading this letter, I was once again sure there
were some good people in this world.

FOUR

The Michelin Plantation

ONE DAY WAS THE SAME AS THE NEXT in Vietnam; there was no real difference between Sunday and Monday. Each day was a day that could decide a man's fate. If it was to be his last say, there were plenty of ways it could happen: a mortar round, a bullet, a Claymore mine that can tear a human body into a thousand pieces, a camouflaged hole in the ground ten feet deep with sharp sticks in the center to pierce his body as he fell into it. We learned to live with death every day; we felt death with us all the time. We didn't think of each day as a day, because it didn't make sense to do so, even though some of us counted the calendar days. We looked forward to one thing—the date we would leave the hell hole of Vietnam and return home. My own departure was far ahead, too far even to think about. Time passed slowly.

One morning I was at my command post when First Sergeant Arthur came in. He pulled up an ammo box and sat down.

"Have you heard yet that all platoon sergeants are to start getting their platoons ready for a move north?" he asked.

"No—what's it all about?"

"I'm not supposed to tell, but you'll find out soon enough when the Old Man is ready to give the word.

Okay?"

"Damn it, you can trust me. After all, I'll be the man up front while you're back here with an operations-map pin in your hand." I smiled, and a small answering smile appeared on Sergeant Arthur's face.

"I'll tell you this much, Vance. We're going north to help the Vietnamese Army get their goddam ass out of hock."

"Help the Vietnamese! What in hell have they fouled up this time?"

"I don't like it any more than you do, but there's not a damn thing we can do about it."

I stood up, and I guess my anger got the better of me. "Us Americans can maybe win this war in the fields. The South Vietnamese leaders and their army may get some support from some of the people, but one thing they never do, and that is to give this miserable country any dignity or self-respect. They don't have the one main factor, the will to help themselves. As long as the Americans are here, the Saigon brass will continue to suck away all they can get. Protection, money, you name it. The people here don't care about us. They only know that we have 'much' money, or so they think."

"Amen," Arthur said.

"After we arrived in this country and I had a chance to see for myself what the place was like, I wrote a poem about it."

"A poem, for Christ's sake!" Arthur said. "What kind of poem?"

"Well, it doesn't rhyme, exactly. They didn't teach

us too much about rhyming back in Douglasville."

"I'm no expert myself. How did it go, if you can remember?"

"Sure, I remember. It's entitled 'Give' and it goes
like this:

"I ask nothing from those of this deprived land.
I give all I have to give in support of freedom.
I do ask this of my fellow countryman
Give half what you have in support of my liberty."

Arthur grinned. "You're on the right track, Vance,
even if it is propaganda, and subversive at that. But try
for some rhymes." His tone changed as he went on. "For
the first few months I guess none of us really knew how
the people felt about us, Vance. But so far all I can see
is that we're only being used."

"On my way here I thought of myself as a black
knight in bright shiny armor going to help a far-off country," I replied. "I felt very patriotic. I respected my leaders, but I felt none of them were superior to me in any
human way, and I felt proud of coming here to do a necessary job. A poor struggling nation was desperately in
need of us. The Americans came to live up to the reputa-
tion as guardians of the world's peace and liberty. That's
how I felt then. Not now."

Arthur nodded. "In my school we had to read some
poems, only they mostly rhymed. One of them was about
a British foul-up and the guy said, 'Theirs not to reason
why, theirs but to do and die.' It's the doing that gets to
me. This way is too fucking much trouble for something

you don't want in the first place." He hunkered down and lit a cigarette. "You're not the only one who feels this way, Vance. A thousand other Americans have the same feeling. I know I do. A man has to be a fool or crazy to want to leave home and fight a war that could be fought without the loss of so many good American guys."

I shook my head. "As you know, I and many other Negroes wanted all this for the chance to prove ourselves. I'm sure you understand that to some degree. But Bau Bang took a lot of my friends. One of them, as he died, said, 'God, it's over.' "

"I'll be glad when this whole damn war is over," Arthur said. "After Bau Bang, we all thought that it would be the last battle for us. Wishful thinking. Anyway, there wasn't anything else to think about that was any better."

"Tell me more about this operation we're getting ready for."

"Well, hell, I may as well, the Old Man's going to, sometime today, anyway. You're going to the Michelin Plantation. Don't say a word about it until the Old Man give all of us the final briefing."

Michelin was one of the largest rubber plantations in the world. "How does the Vietnamese Army fit into this?"

"The Viet Cong surrounded a battalion of the South Vietnamese Army and ordered them to surrender or be destroyed. They surrendered, thinking they wouldn't be harmed, and there were a lot of American advisers in the unit. After the ARVN surrendered, all five hundred of them, the Viet Cong moved in and killed over half of them before support could arrive. They also killed the Americans, which is what our commanders don't want the troops to know. We're going to reinforce what's left of the ARVN. I understand that the Americans in the unit fought like hell and didn't surrender. They kept up the fight until the very last." Arthur looked right at me. "Most of those advisers were Negro."

"If I had a choice, Arthur, the Vietnamese Army could all die," I said.

Arthur let that pass, but then he went on: "The Viet Cong moved in and killed all the advisers first, right in front of the Vietnamese. The Vietnamese who were left, or I should say the ones who survived, were made to swear they would never pick up arms again for either side."

Later that day the company commander gave us the order, and the next morning, in full combat dress, we were moved by assault helicopters to the Michelin Plantation.

We were there for three days without much action. Then, on the third day, I heard the orders. We were going to clear the way from the Michelin Plantation to Ben Cat—about thirty miles—on foot. Marsh's squad was to lead, Kain's would be next, then Roberts, then West, bringing up the rear. My squad leaders were upset about walking the thirty miles; it just didn't seem to make sense. But those were our orders, and that was that.

The first day we walked eight thousand meters—about five miles—loaded down like donkeys going to market. We made camp for the night and set up our front lines as if we expected the Viet Cong, which is always a good idea. The next morning we moved out early.

The code name assigned to our clearing operation back to Ben Cat was "Decoy," and it certainly turned out to be the right designation. On the third morning our orders had us moving down a quiet plantation road, but the quiet was all in the scenery. I was so tense my mouth was dry. Deployed in front of me in strong combat formation was the platoon I had shaped and commanded, good men of whom I was proud. They knew their business and they were certainly aware that we were breaking all the rules, moving along the road as we were.

I watched my men as they moved cautiously ahead, watching everything that moved or appeared to be alive. The squad leaders were controlling their men well. I kept Ben, our radio operator, close beside me, and I could hear snatches of the Old Man's voice talking to the other platoon leaders. Ben and I walked down "ambush alley" like men looking for death. After a while Ben tapped me on the arm and said, "Sarge, why are we walking on this road? We're asking to be ambushed."

"Those are the orders, Ben. We'll follow those orders, which come straight from the battalion commander. Our orders are to let the Viet Cong ambush us."

"Damn! I sure don't like this."

"Me neither, man. If the people back home knew that a crack outfit like ours was being used as bait to make contact with the enemy, they might do some wondering. It might look to them like some of our commanders don't care about lives. They're willing to commit five hundred Americans on a gamble to kill a thousand Viet

Cong. The truth is, three thousand Viet Cong aren't worth one American life."

"*I* know that, but it sure as hell isn't helping us right now. You know, when we passed that little side road a ways back, I'm sure I saw VC firing positions."

"Yeah, I saw them myself."

"This doesn't make any sense at all!" Ben's voice was bitter. "We've been walking for three days, each day doing the same things we did the day before. They taught us never to set patterns, not to do the same thing twice, never walk on roads or trails, because that's where the Viet Cong set their mines. Every day, all day, we walk on roads and trails. Why? Because we're behind time on our march, and our commanders have made bets with other commanders that their troops will make it back befor the others?"

"Is that radio getting heavy, Ben?" I asked. "You hear too much over that radio, and you better be sure you don't repeat what you hear, even if it's true. I got the ass over this operation, too; all the officers in the battalion are disgusted. Most of all they're angry with the battalion commanding officer. All the noncommissioned officers know this, and there's unrest."

"I hope the privates don't hear about it. It's bad enough that I know about it. I wish I didn't."

There was a long way to go before we'd reach base camp. By now, the Viet Cong knew we were there, and they knew where we were going by the pattern we were setting. Our route was plotted so that we'd have to pass almost every clear area between us and the base camp. The

VC weren't fools. When they attacked us, we were going to be caught good. By now we knew they were hunting us. Every morning we had been delayed by snipers, and they were following us all the way. We had lost eight men so far.

Another day and night passed and, before the heat of the following morning reached its peak, our commanders decided to give us a break. We were allowed to sit down in the road and rest for thirty minutes.

All the men I passed were dead on their feet; most of them had stopped right in their tracks. We had very little security out, but everyone was so tired they didn't even care about security. When I stopped by Gibbs's position, he was cleaning his gun.

"That's a smart thing to be doing," I said.

"If you don't clean the piece every day, it'll rust."

"You better get some rest, too."

"How long are we going to stay here, Vance?"

"Only half an hour. If you have any men with foot problems, we'll fly them out tonight."

"Most of my problem boys left during the last two days. A lot of the white boys in this company have had something wrong with them, such as sore feet, headaches, blisters. They're being sent back to the rear. The Negroes are still holding up good. When one guy did say he was sick, we told him he wasn't going to the rear, so he got back in ranks."

"I'm glad only a few of my own men have dropped out, and none of them Negroes."

After four days walking on roads and trails, we

violated *all* the rules we had been taught about jungle warfare. We used old roads and trails that only the Viet Cong and death were allowed to use. We marched on and on, day after day. Some of the men began to fall out from the heat.

I took the radio from Ben and carried it myself; he had gone about as far as he could. He followed right behind me, trying to hold on.

"Sarge," he said almost out of breath, "are we hunting or are we being hunted?"

"Pull yourself together, Ben. You can make it if anybody can," I said, giving him my canteen of water. He had run out the day before, and the Viet Cong hadn't let the resupply choppers land.

The sixth day out, still no real contact, and we were only halfway back. Ben was still making it, but he was still scared, as he should have been.

"Sergeant," he said, "someone had better talk to someone. The men have begun to remember the Battle of Bau Bang and how we met the enemy then on our terms. If he strikes us now, it'll be on his terms."

"Ben, you talk like we'll all be dead before this operation is over. Everyone in this company better pull himself together." As I looked over our formation I realized that if the VC decided to hit us now, we'd have no defense. As we progressed, the men began to lose their nerve; every day someone would barely escape death. By now, too, the men knew there was something going on among the officers. Some even thought the whole unit was falling apart. Still we pushed on under the hot sun, hoping a break would soon come. I wished with all my heart I had never set foot in Vietnam.

The road we were on—or, I should say, the death trap—was long, narrow, and covered with debris. The jungle was heavy and thick on both sides. It was a good place for an ambush. When we stopped for a ten-minute break, I walked over to West. I could see that he was about ready to quit, too.

"I don't like this place at all, Vance," he said to me as I sat down beside him on the half-paved road.

"I don't either. I wish we could get off this road," I replied as I checked my ammunition. In spite of the weight, I always carried eight hundred rounds whenever I went into the field.

Word came back that we were moving again. Some of the men were ready, but some just didn't care one way or the other. The jungle was quiet; the only noise was the tramp of our boots. We must have traveled about three hundred meters when they hit us. Mortar shells fell from the sky like hail and burst all around us. All around there was the loud, thumping sound we had heard at Bau Bang. The fire was like lightning. Bullets came from all directions, and there was very little cover. We were ambushed, and ambushed good, with accuracy and confidence. The Viet Cong were here, here to win.

When the first shot was fired, the whole platoon was jammed up on the road. The second company had just begun to take over from the lead company. We had no advance guard out, no flank security. (That was not important to the commanders, perhaps because a bet had to be won.) The Cong had 50-caliber machine guns in position right in the middle of the road and their heavy machine guns and recoilless rifles were positioned on both sides to cover all possible routes of escape. The men dove to each side of the road for any possible cover.

I made a fast estimate of our situation: it wasn't all bad. We had superior fire power if not manpower. The enemy was striking fast and hard, knowing this was their only chance, and for the first forty minutes they ran the show. They dominated the terrain and the battle, and they tried with all they had to bury all of us then and there. Every bush that moved was shot. Every man who made a sound was shot. We were surrounded.

The wind carried the voices of frightened and dying men. Men were screaming for the medic, but all the medics were dead or close to it. It was as if the Viet Cong could tell the medics from the rest of us. Finally, only one medic was left, and he was mentally incapable of rendering any aid. He fell apart when he saw men dying. He simply couldn't do the job he had been trained for. Half of my platoon had been cut up; the others were doing the best they could with what they had. I had ten men left, and six were Negroes. Our commanding officer was only fifty meters away, but he might as well have been a thousand. A 50-caliber had him pinned down, and the only thing *he* could do was sit tight.

The company commander had every reason to be angry. His company was being hurt the worst. He radioed the battalion commander, who was flying high above in an aircraft, studying the war no doubt. We could hear the exchange on our radio.

"Colonel, you got us into this. Goddam it, you get us out."

"You're not the only one down there, Captain, and you watch your mouth," the batallion commander replied. The battle raged on. The smell of death was in the air.

"Bring all the wounded onto the road," shouted a voice from the jungle.

"Sarge, bring the wounded onto the road," one of the squad leaders from the other platoon said.

"Who said so, LeRoy?"

"Someone from up front; they're trying to get them out of here."

"Wait, wait—before you put the wounded out in the open, find out who gave that order," I yelled.

But before I could get through to him, all the wounded from the third platoon were on the road, and before they knew what was happening the Viet Cong killed them all. It was the Viet Cong who had given the order to move the wounded onto the road.

"Over your head, Sergeant—VC!" a voice shouted at me.

I turned over on my back and fired into the top of a tree. When I fired the final shot, a bloody body fell down. Meanwhile, men from all over were calling for first aid.

Screaming, the VC fired on us from all corners of the ambush site. As we were trying to keep them off us, the radio squawked.

"Sergeant Vance," the company commander called.

"Look out. There's about thirty Cong coming down on your side. You're right in their path."

By this time I had been hit, but two men beside me were wounded very badly. "Richard, try and keep Paul quiet. I know he's hurt, but do whatever you can."

"My God! When will we get out of here?" Paul cried.

"Hold it down," I demanded. "I can hear them."

The VC were walking fast toward us, and we had no place to run or hide, even if we wanted to. We had to stay there. Heavy firing started again and the jets made it almost unbearable. If we're still alive when this is over we can only thank God, I thought. I was scared.

The VC saw us first and opened up. We fired back, but most of the time we couldn't see our targets. They could see some of us but not all of us, and they rushed us, screaming.

"Cover right, Richard!" I yelled, but he didn't hear me. His eyes were trained on the black uniforms and his trigger finger was locked in his machine gun. "In front of you Sarge! Watch it, watch it!"

As the VC ran toward me, I hit him twice on full automatic, and he hit me. It was over for him and almost for me. The bullet cut my chest but didn't penetrate. It didn't hurt at first but then it started burning.

Paul had been hit again and was in horrible pain. Half his mouth had been blown away. His words were broken and unclear but he could be heard for miles: "Help me, mother, please help me," he cried. Then his twisting body was still. His pain was over.

I had lost half of my platoon. I was the only Negro

platoon sergeant, and we had more Negro soldiers than any other platoon in the company. And we had been the lead platoon when the ambush hit. You can't help remembering facts like that.

The battle lasted for eight hours. The Viet Cong withdrew only after the Air Force finally came in and dropped five-hundred-pound bombs on their positions. We found our wounded scattered all through the jungle around us.

Late that night we began policing up. We put all the dead we could find in one place. We had a stack of damaged weapons that would have taken a hundred men to carry, so we had to leave them. Gibbs had finished bringing all the dead men out of the jungle in his area to the road. When I found him leaning on his rifle in a corner of the jungle he seemed to have reserved for himself, I asked, "Gibbs, how do you feel?"

"Not so good, Sarge. I've watched too many of my friends die, and for what? I've had my share. How's your wound? It looks bad."

"Don't get excited. Things'll be all right," I said, almost automatically. "Did you get all the wounded and dead out?"

"I think so. There were so many that I don't really know. It'll take three hours to get them all out of the jungle and onto the road. After that we have to get them to the landing strip, and that's five hundred meters down the road."

"It's not going to be easy, but we'll do it."

"I hope so," he said.

In spite of all our care and work, we left one live man behind overnight. When we came back to the ambush site the next morning to fly the dead out, we found him. We also found that the bodies had been stripped of their wedding bands and all other valuables.

Pfc. Simon, a tall, heavy-set dark Negro from Alabama, was one of my automatic riflemen, and there wasn't anything he didn't do to help. All the boys loved him. Simon worked like a madman trying to get men out of the jungle. He and about three other Negroes managed to get the majority of the wounded out, and during the action he had killed three Viet Cong that he knew of.

This time we had really got our taste of action, more than we ever dreamed of. The unit was so beat that the batallion was declared unable to complete its mission. We were no longer effective as a fighting force. I waited until the last chopper load to leave, and the Old Man had to force me to go then. My wound was nothing compared to those of some of the other men. I only stayed three days in the hospital, and it seemed like no time at all before I was back in the company area.

It was unusually quiet in the camp. Everyone was waiting for replacements—we had time to remember.

A day or two later I was relaxing at the mess hall after chow when Sergeant LeRoy and Sergeant Davis came over and sat down. And with both of them were the pains of war. The three of us sat there; no one moved, no one spoke.

"Talking about things sometimes helps," I said.

"Depressed as we are, how long can we go on?" LeRoy said curtly.

I said nothing.

"But we should maybe talk. Tomorrow, the next day, or the one after that, we'll be going out again. So we should talk now, while we've got the chance," Davis suggested.

Sergeant Arthur came over and joined us. He hadn't been on the operation, and he was eager to hear firsthand reports. "How long were you out before you were ambushed?" he asked.

LeRoy answered: "We'd been in the field for a lot of days, more days than a man should have to stay out. Every day the sniper fire was getting heavier. Every time we moved we were fired upon. The Viet Cong seemed to know what we were going to do before we did. On this operation, we did things, on order, that we had been drilled never to do—for instance, never rush in or hurry so much that security wouldn't be effective. But we *did* rush in, and if we hadn't been in such a hurry we wouldn't have had to pull our security out of the jungle and walk down that damn road without our eyes and ears."

"People think the Viet Cong are crazy, but they're crazy like foxes," I said. "Another thing, we've always been told never to set patterns, but our commanders gave us a schedule that we had to follow every day. In the afternoon around 1530 hours we would set up our batallion perimeter. At approximately 1600 hours the resupply helicopter would come in. Every morning around 0730 hours we would send our support weapons in, and every time we did that we received sniper fire until we moved out for that day. That was the schedule. We were ordered to use it every day until the battle."

"That's right," Davis said. "And just before the attack I had my squad on the right side of the formation, providing flank security. I spotted fresh-dug foxholes and different things made out of wood. When I reported this to the platoon leader, he told me to keep my eyes open. He's dead now, but not because my eyes weren't open."

"I remember that," LeRoy broke in. "That's when we got the word to take over the lead from B Company, and as we started to pass through we got hit from the front and both flanks. We were caught in cross-fire. If the batallion hadn't been in such a hurry, the flank security could have picked up the Cong dug in along the road. Most of the people who were killed and wounded were hit by the first fire. If the VC had waited a few more minutes they would've had the whole batallion, would've cleaned us out completely. God knows I was scared, and so were my men. One of the things that bugged us was that we didn't know where the Cong were or where we could fire without killing our own men."

Davis said: "Overall, the men did an outstanding job in lots of ways. There was this Negro soldier beside me from another company and we'd said we were going to make it through this if we had to kill every Viet Cong out there by ourselves. He fought with everything he had before he was killed.

"But when I think of Sergeant Curtis it makes my stomach hurt; he came crawling back to the rear, scared to death. He didn't know where his men were, or if they had been wounded or killed, and he didn't try to find them. He forgot them completely. I watched him crawling like the lowest thing in the world. He'll catch plenty of hell just being with the other men. But then there was Private Weaver, who was with the platoon leader when he was killed. Weaver picked up the radio that had been blown off the platoon leader's back and tried to find someone to take over. He crawled along the entire right flank of the platoon, under heavy fire."

A number of the Negro noncommissioned officers had got into the habit of reviewing combat situations and the way things were going, and it was almost like a club. White sergeants seldom joined us, and we didn't ask them. It wasn't hard to understand why. We had something in common, our color, that went far deeper even than the war itself. We had something to prove, and it was a tough thing to establish.

If you belong to a race that is regarded by many of your countrymen as inferior, it's not enough to demonstrate that you are just as good as they are. You have to prove you're better just to get an equal chance. But there's a danger in that, too, that you'll be hated or distrusted for making the other guy look inferior in comparison. I thought back to my talk with Gilbert on the transport coming over. I sure had sounded confident then. I still felt sure of my own position, but in a different way.

We Negroes were fighting two wars at once—the Vietnam war, and the war for our own dignity and equality. If any one of us failed the test of combat, he let all the rest of us down. The white soldiers didn't have the rest of their race riding on their shoulders. I knew that there were black heroes in all the battle records in all American wars, but this was the first full-scale war in an integrated army, and we surely were being watched and tested. We were under extra pressure—all of us, from Colonel Smoke on down to me and every Negro private.

Sitting there in the humid heat of a Vietnam evening and talking with friends of the same color who were under the same strains and tensions it was easy to feel something more than disgust about Sergeant Curtis and his failure to meet the ultimate test. In a way, it was almost easy to feel relief. A white man had chickened out and a black man had not. A black man had actually saved the scene, and made the white man look bad by comparison. There was a kind of comfort in that. But I started out with more white soldiers than black under my command, and the failure of any one man, white or black, was a failure of the unit and a danger to everybody.

Finally, I decided that even though Curtis was a white man and even though he'd showed yellow in the action, he was just a misfit in this war, he didn't belong here. He wasn't a failure just because he was white.

Lightning bugs were flickering around us as we sat there, but they only made the night a blacker kind of hell. While the others were talking, I was thinking that in war darkness and the night befriend no one. We always felt that the Viet Cong were night people, and that the dark was their half of the twenty-four hours, when they came back to their villages, or moved their troops, or laid their ambushes. Perhaps they were out there not too far away doing all those things. And yet, maybe they thought the darkness befriended *us*, covering our movements, concealing our predawn ambush patrols, hiding the threat of us from them.

Then we got to talking about some of the men who had been wounded in the battle.

"Did you see Sergeant Cox?" Davis asked. "He was on the last load, I think."

"No. He was on the chopper before me. When I got on mine, I felt sorry for the men with me. Some had lost arms or legs or eyes, but they were so glad to get away from there that their wounds didn't seem to matter to them. They were just glad to be out of it alive."

LeRoy dropped his head and said, "Yeah. There were four men beside me that day who were wounded real bad, and just listening to them was too much for me."

"On the chopper I found myself thinking of my own wounds, almost, sometimes, with joy. I knew I had caught it just enough to get me off the front lines and safe into the hospital. But 'way down inside I wanted to stay with my men, come hell or high water."

"I know what you mean," Davis said.

"It's bad," I went on, "but when we finally lifted off the ground, out of reach of small-arms fire, I felt a sense of security, like a child when his mother saves him from a bad fall. I knew I was lucky to be alive, and that I had God to thank for it. It wasn't long before we got in the big hospital in Saigon."

"Did you see your old platoon sergeant there?" Arthur asked, getting ready to leave. "Rogers, I mean?"

"I saw old Rogers. I'll tell you about him later. So, after seeing the doctor, I settled down in a nice, soft bed between two cool white sheets. It was almost like being in heaven, after being in the dirt for eight days. I looked at all the people around wearing clean clothes and I wondered if they lived like this all the time."

"Hell, those asses down there don't even know there's a war going on," Davis said.

"That's right, and most of them are white. Very few Negroes."

"Don't tell us that, man. Anywhere there's a soft life you can forget looking for the black boys," said LeRoy resentfully.

Arthur chuckled and said, "Being there, a man could almost feel sure he'd make it home alive."

"When I looked at my underclothes they were so dirty, they were almost as dark as I am."

"Hell with it," remarked LeRoy. "We had gone without clean clothes for thirteen entire days."

"Yeah, but after seeing everyone else clean, I was a little ashamed of my condition. The next morning when I saw the nurse I thought for sure I was in heaven. I almost went into shock just looking at her. She had blonde hair, blue eyes, and very soft-looking skin. Her voice sounded like a harp. And the best thing about her was that she was an American, with round eyes."

"Oh, man! Don't say any more. It's been a long time since I've had a real woman," said Arthur.

"I almost forgot that a lot of our people got lynched not too long ago on account of women like her, but I didn't think about that for very long. Then I talked to some of the other fellows and found out that some of them had figured out angles to keep from going back to the lines, and I was tempted to write to the President. That's when I saw Sergeant Rogers; he was still in the hospital with a minor wound. Right away he began telling me about it, as if I was wondering why it was taking him so long to back to the platoon. I also found out he'd been lying to the doctor so he could stay in the hospital longer."

Arthur said grimly: "That's the kind of man the Army should kill. People like him and Curtis."

"They'll have their day. He's the kind of sergeant who's had seventeen years' service, and to talk to him you'd think he was the whole Army. His kind lives and sleeps the Army while there's no war, but comes the day when they have to earn their pay in battle, they turn into fat nothings."

It was late, but they kept after me to hear the rest of the hospital story. I told them it was short and sweet. I had been in the hospital for only three days and on one of them I was awarded the Purple Heart. I couldn't help feeling proud when the General Westmoreland, the commander of all the U.S. forces in Vietnam, pinned the medals on us.

"Were you in bed when the general came around?" LeRoy asked.

"No, I was able to stand, but a lot of the other guys

couldn't. When he walked in and stopped in front of me, you better believe I snapped to attention. His four stars were shining in my eyes.

" 'When the commander walks in front of you, sound off with your name and rank loud and clear,' a voice said from behind us.

"So I sounded off: 'Sir, Staff Sergeant Samuel Vance.'

"He asked me how I was doing, and I told him I was doing fine. Then he asked me where I had been wounded and what battle I was in."

When General Westmoreland had finished with us he went on to some of the other men who weren't as lucky as we had been. Walking back to my ward, I thought of these other soldiers who paid a far higher price for their Purple Hearts.

Staying in the hospital was eating hot meals every day, sleeping between clean sheets every night, not having to worry about getting bugs in my ears from sleeping in foxholes filled with water. When I first came to the hospital, I had thirteen days of pure dirt on me. I was used to eating cold combat rations. Now I was clean and eating hot food every day, starting to feel like a man again. All these things made the hospital almost like home. I didn't want to think about going back to the field. No one did.

But still, after the third day, I was on the way back to my platoon. The foxholes were still there, the mud, the water and ants, everything I left was still here. I turned to Sergeant Davis and said, "Including you."

Davis said, "Sorry about that, Vance. You should

have known the easy life was not for you."

"That's right," Arthur broke in. "And I'm going to bed. You three cats can stay out here and talk all night if you want, but not me."

FIVE

We Stand with
the Brave

THE COMBAT SOLDIER is blessed if the war stops for a second. For the black soldier there's no end. A fight is the same—different country and different weapons, that's all. The next morning orders came for a new operation. It was good to be in command again. The hospital had been nice, but I belonged here. The Old Man called me to the command post.

"Pull up a box, Vance, and sit down," he said when I entered.

As soon as I was settled he got down to business.

"I have a very important mission, and it has to be led by the best leader I have. That's why you're here."

"Just what is this mission, sir?" I paused and then decided to go ahead. "As you know, sir, I was the leader of the last 'very important mission' you had." My voice sounded positive.

"I'm aware of that, Sergeant, but this is also important to the battalion commander. I have no choice." He sounded sympathetic but firm—very firm.

"May I talk to you man to man, Captain Berger?"

"If it's necessary, Vance, yes, you may."

"Frankly, I feel that I and all other Negro noncommissioned officers are being used for these rough assignments because we've tried harder to do our jobs."

"Why don't you come right out with it?" The captain's voice rose and his face began to redden. "You think that because you're Negro, you're being used. Is that it?"

"Yes! That's the way I really feel. Don't get me wrong, Captain. I'm not crying, because I know there isn't a job in this company that I can't do well. I was beginning to get angry and the commander must have realized it. "What I can't understand is how you can allow the white sergeants to cool their heels so much—why should *we* have to lead all the bad missions? To me, as long as a man is a sergeant he should earn his pay or take his rank and give it to someone else."

"I'm going to say this, Sergeant Vance, and the matter is going to be closed. You have a patrol tomorrow night."

But I was too angry to stop. "I just want to say one last thing to you, sir. I used to have a lot of respect for you but now, as far as I'm concerned, you're not worth a goddam."

The captain's eyes narrowed. "Just who the hell do you think you are, Sergeant? I'm aware of your popularity in this battalion, but I'm the company commander and I'll control the unit as I see fit. Here are your orders, Sergeant Vance. Now act accordingly."

I took my orders and returned to my platoon. I was so damn angry I could hardly speak.

"Ben, have all the squad leaders report to me."

"You want them right now?"

"Yes, and tell them to make it fast." Minutes later they were in the command post, and I explained our operation. "Our mission, men, is to move out of this area under the cover of darkness. Four squads. Full combat gear. We will surround, now hear me good, we will surround the village of Bau Vin Long and during first light we will attempt to capture the village chief."

Angrily, West said, "Who in hell thought up a crazy operation like that? And how come *we* get the mission?"

"God help us, is all I have to say," Roberts said, jerking his head.

"Let's hear the rest of it, Sarge," Ben said.

"Well, they seem to think this chief is a Viet Cong battalion commander under cover."

"What's your plan, Sarge?" Kain said.

"Here's how we'll try to do it." They all gathered around to make sure they understood the plan of operation.

We'd been in and around our target village at least a hundred times and knew every inch of it, and we all knew the order of march from there. When the point squad reached the small stream on the north side of the village, we would stop and put out security. Kain was to clear the other side by sending one man across to serve as a listening post. His squad was to be deployed for the scout's fast recovery. If we were detected, we were to pull back and call the mission off.

The first squad would move north of Vin Long, second squad would cover the southwest end, and the third squad would hold the northeast side. Since the river was to the south we didn't need to worry about that. Before first light West would have two machine guns in place to cover the entire village. Fourth squad would occupy Bau

Vin Long at first light. A 0430 Kain would move down to the chief's hut and if the chief was inside, get him out and bring him back. All Kain would need was one fire team because he'd be covered topside.

To get back to base camp we'd meet at the stream; if all squads weren't there by 0530 each squad was to infiltrate back to the camp.

At sundown we moved out. The jungle was very dark and quiet as we slowly made our way toward Bau Vin Long. Three hours later we were in position.

"We didn't have any problems on the way, Sarge. I hope it stays that way for the rest of this crazy mission," Roberts said in a whisper.

"So do I, Rob. It's too close to Christmas."

At first light we prepared to execute the last phase of our plan. Quietly I asked over the radio: "Are your guns in place, West?"

He answered: "All's well."

"Are you moving, Kain?"

"Yes, we're on our way."

They made their way down the hill toward the chief's hut. We waited in silence; everything seemed to be going well. Suddenly the silence was broken by rifle fire. We could see people beginning to mill around.

"Hold your fire!" Kain yelled.

"They got James, Sarge," one of his men cried.

"I got the chief, Paul, bring up the rear!" Kain shouted back.

Adding to the confusion was the sound of an explosion and, with it, death screams.

"Someone help us!" one of the men cried.

Clearly the situation was bad, but I was too far away for accurate appraisal. "West, cover me. I'm going down there. Take over the platoon and give us ten minutes before you move out."

"All right. We'll fire over you. Maybe that'll keep their heads down."

I stumbled down the hill, heading toward the confusion, guided by the cries of the wounded men. I found two of our people; they were dead. Then I found three other bodies; those were Viet Cong.

"Kain! Kain!" I called.

"Over here, Sarge! This way!"

When I found Kain he was trying to drag the unconscious chief back up the hill. Two of Kain's men found us and gave us a hand.

"What happened, Kain?"

"The chief had three bodyguards outside his hut. We killed two, but one is still around."

We were almost up the hill when we heard: "Damn GI's, you die! You die, GI's!"

Right after that there was the crack of a rifle, and I felt the sting in my shoulder, then the burning.

Calmly, I said to Kain, "I'm hit," and then passed out.

"How do you feel Sarge?" someone beside me said.

"Okay, I guess. I'm a little sore, but not too much."

After a month in the hospital, I was ready to go back to my platoon.

Christmas was near, and the nurses had begun to decorate the hospital. The tiny Vietnamese Red Cross girls came around and brought nice things and said nice things, trying hard to make us all feel at home.

I was standing outside the door of our ward with a Negro platoon sergeant named Bob who had been wounded by a land mine, when the Vietnamese Red Cross girls found us. They came up and said, "We give you this gift on behalf of all the Vietnamese people. We want you to know that we are very proud and grateful for what you are doing for us." They handed us each a small package.

Their words were good to hear, and I was grateful for what they were trying to do.

"So, what do you think of them now, Bob?"

He shook his head. "I thought of all the good men who died by my side. These people speak the same language as the Viet Cong. There's nothing anyone in this country can do to make me feel at home."

"I used to feel that way too, but after watching those kids with the Red Cross, I feel a little different." Bob didn't answer.

"Remember," I said to him, "when the Vietnamese kids played American songs and we cheered? Some of the men even cried. It made some of us glad to see children trying to do something to make us feel better and prove that someone in this country cares about us."

Bob shook his head again. "It's only the real small children, if anyone."

"When do you leave here? Have you had the word yet?"

"No, not yet, but any day now," he said. "We have

to go back if we're able to. We have a job, and that's what we're here for."

"I know, but there are plenty of GI's who say they're not going back north. A lot of them keep telling the doctor they're not well enough to go back."

"Well, you don't see me or any of the other brothers doing that. Most of the men who refuse to go back are whites."

Bob left the hospital a day or so later and went back to the First Division. I had a few more days left in the hospital. Christmas came, and my Christmas was better than what most soldiers had in Vietnam. I had no complaints.

Harold, one of my men, wrote to me while I was in the hospital and told me what was going on in the platoon, which made me feel really good. Harold was relatively new in the outfit. In bed, before the lights were turned out, I read his letter over again. The first part of the letter was about the platoon and some small fire fights. Then he wrote, "Sergeant, I wrote to my mother and told her what my Christmas was like on the front lines in Vietnam, and I thought you might be interested in what I had to say:

" 'On Christmas Eve I was 300 meters behind the front lines of my platoon near Lai Khe. Our company had just returned from a nine-hour sweep through the thick, hot, infested jungle. We couldn't be happy because two of our men had been killed. They were so close to the time when our Savior, Jesus Christ, was born. They never made it, not alive, not on this earth.

" 'After chow, we went back to our bunkers on the line, the place where we will live for the next twelve months. Fifty meters to our front are rows of barbed wire, mines, booby traps, and tin cans, all to let us know in advance if the enemy is coming. Beyond the wires and mines is the enemy, waiting for a moment to make his strike; but he'll only make it if he's sure of victory.

" 'I was very lonely on Christmas eve as I stood guard while my bunkmate slept. There was no tree to decorate, no presents to wrap. I thought not of the dying, not of the death that could come at any time, but of the first Christmas many centuries ago, when our Savior was born. Despite the holiday cease-fire, the Viet Cong still crawls up to our barbed wire to harass us, and as usual they switch their flashlights on and walk around the area trying to make us nervous. That night the Viet Cong didn't fire at us and we didn't fire at them. After my watch was up I went to sleep. Christmas Eve was the first night I've spent in Vietnam that I didn't fall asleep to the sounds of heavy guns firing all night and occasionally the chatter of our machine gun.

" 'Then it was Christmas morning—a morning such as I'd never experienced in all my life. We had nothing to give, nothing to receive, nothing at all. But in each of us we felt the true Christmas spirit.

" 'That morning we heard the old familiar sound, the call for chow, and we walked, as always, to the mess hall area, only to find the same old breakfast—powdered eggs, dried bacon, crackers. Again, as for the past five days, I couldn't eat that stuff they call food. I filled my helmet with hot water and carried it back to the place I call home so I could wash as well as possible. I haven't had a bath in three weeks.

" 'About an hour later my friends and I went to the chapel for Christmas services. Walking along the muddy road, beating off the mosquitoes, we came to the old bombed-out building with a big white cross in front that is the chapel. We prayed, and thanked God that we were alive to see Christmas Day. Then we returned to the company area, where we had a company formation and our battalion commander presented Purple Hearts to the men who had been wounded. When the formation was over, we had Christmas dinner, and for the first time since Thanksgiving, we had a real good meal. We were also given cold beer, compliments of the CBS crew. They made a film of our company they're calling *Christmas in Vietnam.*

" 'The rest of the day we just sat around the platoon area and listened to the radio, which was playing Christmas music. We all enjoyed Christmas Day, but it was nothing like home. Even though the enemy wasn't shooting at us, we knew he wasn't far away, looking, listening, waiting.

" 'Tonight the cease-fire will be over, and the war will start again. We have to turn our thoughts from holiday dreams to the world of death and destruction. We want so much for this to end so we can go home to our families and loved ones. Just a few lines to let you know how I feel on Christmas Day, Mom.' "

When I had finished rereading the letter I was proud of Harold. He was a good man and a real soldier. Real soldiers are guys with a lot of heart.

Not long after Christmas I returned to Lai Khe and took up my duties as platoon leader. When I first came to Vietnam, I was the weapons-squad leader, but in a war zone, one day you're a rifleman and the next you're the platoon leader. That's the way it goes, and you can't win them all.

Most of the men in my platoon were new replacements, but there were some familiar faces.

"It's good to have you back, Vance," Sergeant Gibbs said. "We have a lot of new men, and they're *really* new—fresh out of the States. They been told you'd be back, but most of them don't know you're Negro."

"That's no problem, Gibbs. I'll take care of that."

I passed some of the new men in the platoon area, and they were obviously surprised to see I was Negro.

"Say, Vance!" Kain yelled from his position. "It's good to have you back. How's the shoulder?"

"It's okay. How's everything?"

"All right. We've been waiting for you."

All of the old men were glad to see me, and they welcomed me back to the best platoon in the United States Army. I let a few days pass to give the new men a chance to get used to seeing me around. Then on my third day back I called a meeting of all the new men. I wanted to let them know just how they stood with me and what to expect for the next twelve months. I planned to make men of them and see that most of them got back home. They looked nervous and clearly didn't know what to expect at the meeting. By then I had learned most of their names but there were still one or two I didn't know. They came from all over the United States—New York, California, Kentucky, Mississippi . . .

"I want to welcome all of you to the best platoon in the United States Army. I'm sure all of you are familiar with the record behind this unit." They were all looking right at me. My beginning seemed to surprise them.

I knew, of course, that they were just out of training, and while I wanted to make them feel at home, I also wanted to let them know they were far away from their own homes and had to pull their own weight. They had to act, think, and *be* men if they wanted to survive.

"I am the leader of this platoon, and I don't want any of you to forget that. I know you're all well trained physically and mentally, and capable of handling the jobs you're going to be assigned. You came here to do one big job as fighting men, and all of you are going to do that job." Some of them dropped their heads, but some continued to look right at me—I liked that.

"I want you to remember this. You may be the best-trained men in the world, but some of you are going to die here in Vietnam because that's the way God intended for it to be. Face up to that.

"Now, it's our job to try and complete any mission we are assigned. We have done just that in the past, and we're going to keep on doing it. As of this day, men, you will no longer be referred to as the new men in this platoon."

I kept my voice firm and commanding. I wanted them to understand that this place called Vietnam was no place to relax, because if you did you would be killed. I meant for them to hear and to understand, and before I was through they did. I talked about things they would be confronted with while in the first platoon. We discussed rank, the chain of command, respect for leaders, and I pointed out a great number of things involved in fighting the Viet Cong. When I was through I felt sure they believed they were in good hands as far as leadership was concerned.

"That's all for now," I concluded. "Just don't forget what I've told you."

Then I was alone again, thinking about an earlier fire fight, and the platoon leader we had had then. A day, an hour, or a week from now, would I still be here, or would it be another noncommissioned officer talking to the men as I just had?

Later I was talking to my close friend, Gilbert, who asked me if I'd heard about Sergeant Wright.

"No. What happened to him?"

"He got it last week on an operation in War Zone C."

"Oh, my God! I didn't know."

Gilbert's eyes looked heavy.

"Who's the platoon leader up there now?"

"A new sergeant just in from the States." He was silent for a moment. "No one will ever take Wright's place. He was a man of men—a man you'd never forget once you'd met him."

"I never knew him that well, but I saw him operate a number of times. He was good, all right."

"I'll miss him. So will all the other men in our platoon. All of us Negro noncoms should really be proud of him. He was a career soldier with eighteen years' service. He was forty-three and he must have weighed 220 pounds, and he was a well-educated man who spoke well. He was a wonderful man, strange in lots of ways, loved by everyone except those who only wanted to compete with him and couldn't. Yeah, Wright was full of fire. We almost believed he could lick the world alone."

As Gilbert talked, it almost felt like Sergeant Wright was there. "I had just come back from jungle training in Hawaii," Gilbert continued, "when I first met Wright at Fort Devens. At that time Grant was our platoon sergeant, another decorated soldier, also a Negro. When I was introduced to Wright, for some reason I got the impression he was irresponsible, but I didn't make a final judgment. Anyway, to look at Wright you felt there was something strange about him. Before leaving the States, the two of us had time to get acquainted. Maybe it was sharing the training. That training was hard, even if no one really learned much from it."

"Boy, you don't have to tell me about the training at Devens. I know we didn't learn very damn much."

"I'll never forget some of those exercises," Gilbert said. "During night training platoons were crossing in front of each other as they moved through dark woods that were supposed to simulate the jungles of South Vietnam. If it'd been real we would've been firing on each other!" Gilbert snorted.

"Wright had been around for a long time and he knew the ropes. When he walked he walked tall and proud, and his voice had authority; you never forgot it. Well, anyhow, when the training tapered off, we had a little time to do some running around. Every day—even during duty hours—Wright would go down to the local bar and have a few drinks. He could drink double shots one right after the other and never get drunk. He could drink more than any man I ever knew. And the most amazing thing was that he could get up in the morning, after drinking all night, and take physical training with the rest of us even though he was in his forties. He ran for five miles with all us young guys and kept right up. It was something.

"That was the beginning of my experience with 'Number 1'—we all called him that because he was the squad leader of the first squad. He pretended he didn't like it, but we knew he did. He used to tell us not to call him that because if we did it then, when we got to Vietnam the first man who'd be called on when a patrol had to go out would be him—'Number 1.' I laughed, since I didn't think it would really happen.

"We were all overworked and beat at Devens, but worse was to come. Some of us knew it, and some of us just didn't care. Wright and I often talked, but there were times when he'd start to tell me something and then, right in the middle, he'd stop.

"By the time we reached Vietnam, I had grown fond

of old 'Number 1.' I covered up for him sometimes when the platoon sergeant was looking for him and he had cut out for the local village. Most of us in the platoon thought the world of him. Wright was a leader, and most of the time he was happy, laughing, and making others laugh. That helped take our minds off of home.

"When Wright died in the middle of the jungle, I thought of the times, when things were hard, that he'd say to us: 'Drive on men, just drive right on.' I also remembered something he said as we were getting to Okinawa. When I asked him what he was thinking, he answered: 'As we approach this remote island I feel a sense of history, of reliving the past. What a price we Americans had to pay for this tiny piece of land. I wonder what those men were thinking when they made their assault here years ago? What did the commanders feel when they heard, or gave, the orders to lower the landing craft? What did the soldier feel when his landing craft touched the beach? Now I wonder if, when we reach Vietnam, I'll feel the same way they did.' "

SIX

A Father,
a Son,
and War

THE BATTALION COMMANDER stood at attention; the division commander was standing on his right with his two silver stars shining in the sun. Men who had distinguished themselves during the battle of the Michelin Plantation were standing in formation in front of the commanders. I was one of them—the first man, in fact. In front of us was the jungle's edge, and beyond that line, somewhere, were the Viet Cong. From far away came the sound of our big guns. We heard the roar of fighter jets on their way to harass the enemy. I was being recommended for the nation's third-highest award—the Silver Star—and the Purple Heart. Before the commander presented the medal, the orders were read. Under the tropical sun the words were deeply solemn:

"The following award has been made to Staff Sergeant Samuel Vance: The Silver Star for gallantry in action.

"Staff Sergeant Samuel Vance distinguished himself, on 5 December 1965, while serving as the platoon leader to a unit on a battalion search-and-destroy operation in the vicinity of Ap Nha Mat, the Michelin Plantation, Republic of Vietnam. The units had been sweeping through the jungle for seven days and had sustained numerous casualties from Viet Cong delaying forces. At approximately

1230 hours, the battalion contacted an estimated four well-entrenched Viet Cong battalions. The friendly forces were brought under intensive mortar, recoilless rifle, .50-caliber machine gun, and automatic weapons fire by a numerically superior Viet Cong force."

I was proud as I listened to my commander's voice, and also, perhaps, surprised in a curious, unexpected way. I had never talked about what I had done during the battle, since I wasn't sure I deserved an award.

The commander went on: "During the initial attack, his three squad leaders were mortally wounded. Without hesitation and with complete disregard for his own personal safety, Staff Sergeant Vance exposed himself to intense hostile fire to control his platoon. Moving from position to position, he ignored the intense hostile fire to direct the fire of his platoon into the midst of the fiercely counterattacking Viet Cong. During the course of action, Staff Sergeant Vance, again with complete disregard for his personal safety, while exposed to the hostile fire, went to the aid of the wounded artillery forward observer who had been mortally wounded by the hostile fire. While moving him to a covered position, Staff Sergeant Vance was painfully wounded. Although wounded, he adjusted artillery fire and air strikes in support of his embattled platoon, and assisted in aiding and evacuating other wounded comrades of his unit

"Staff Sergeant Vance's aggressiveness, devotion to duty, and personal bravery inspired his men to increase their efforts, which added immeasurably to defeat of a numerically superior Viet Cong force. Staff Sergeant

Vance's unimpeachable valor in close combat against a Viet Cong force was in keeping with the highest traditions of the military service and reflects great credit upon himself, his unit, and the United States Army."

With military efficiency, the citations were all read and the medals presented. We were dismissed, and I wandered over to have a few words with my comrade Sergeant Shanklen, who had just received the Bronze Star for his part in the action of Bau Bang. He was looking at the medal, and as I came up to him I saw him throw it away.

"What did you do that for?" I asked him.

Shanklen's face was bitter. "I don't want nothing to remind me of that damned night when half my squad was killed."

"But the medal is for *your* action," I said. "You ought to be proud of that."

He stared back at me. "No," he said flatly. "No. I don't want anything they have to give me but my freedom."

Even before the awards ceremony a number of us had received orders and briefing, and ten hours later my platoon was airborne and on its way to make an assault landing somewhere in the Delta; the operation was designated "Bull Run." In spite of a lot of previous experience with air operations of this sort, our hearts were heavy; we disliked the prospect of unfamiliar terrain and combat situations in which we were going inevitably to find ourselves at a disadvantage.

We came in for the landing, and it was all too familiar. Our stomachs were full of knots and our rear ends tightened up. The choppers had come in at tree top level; they landed in the center of the zone and in a matter of seconds we were unloaded and headed toward the jungle for security. The choppers took off again, and we were alone. When you watched them go like that you felt you were crying inside.

The soldier next to me as we slogged across the wet, muddy rice paddies toward the jungle edge, was named Calvin. He had been in the platoon about six months, but in that time he had made a place for himself. All the men had come to like him, and although he was white, the Negroes had come to treat him as if he were one of us. Wherever the black soldiers went, Calvin was right with them.

He turned to me. "How long are we going to be out here, Sarge?" Calvin asked cheerfully.

"I wish I knew," I said.

Finally we got across the rice paddies, established our perimeter on the north side of the area, and began to dig in, each man in his assigned position. Later I went out to check all positions, and on my way back to the command post I came to Calvin's foxhole. He had been hard at work.

"Do you think that hole is deep enough, Calvin?" I asked him innocently.

Calvin smiled and answered: "It's almost over my head now, Sarge."

"Well, the platoon is in position, so if old Charlie is looking for a fight we'll be here waiting on him."

"How many Viet Cong are we looking for?"

"This operation is supposed to break the back of the enemy."

"That's what they always say. This one will turn out just like the others."

I sat down beside Calvin as night came on. "This part of the day is beautiful," he said. "After seeing this, you wonder how could this land be so full of war."

"There are many wonders to be seen here, Calvin. By the way, when's the last time you heard from your father?"

"I had a letter from him last week; he's still talking about the same old thing. You know, Sarge, I've told you quite a lot about my life, but you've only told me a little bit about yours."

The moon was full and the light shone on Calvin's face, with his dark shiny hair curled all over his head.

"I think I've told you as much about myself as I've told anyone else."

"I know. I just said that because I felt you were tired of hearing my life story." Calvin closed his eyes for a second and took a deep breath.

"What's really bothering you, Calvin?"

"I never told you why I came into the Army, did I?"

"No, not really. You did say something about your father, but that's all."

"I came into the Army to get away from my old man and the so-called life I had. You asked me once before why I came in when I was twenty-six but didn't go to OCS. Well, I didn't know what I wanted out of life. My father, with his influence, kept me out of the service until I decided the only way I could maintain my sanity was to join the Army."

"I bet you didn't bank on coming to Vietnam, huh?" I was ashamed of the remark the instant I had made it, but Calvin took it as natural.

"Yes, I did. I asked for Infantry and war duty here. I'd gone from one school to another and my father has enough money to buy Vietnam, but he has another problem. Have you ever heard of a Barker family in New York City?"

"No, I haven't spent much time in New York."

"Sometimes I think I hate my father. Our chauffeur was more like a father to me, and I loved him. He was Negro but to me he was love, and a buddy. He made up for my father."

"What was it made you leave home?"

"In my home there were the people who ran the house, people like Neal, the chauffeur, and Jennie, the maid, and a few others who were a part of the Barker family. I had everything a boy could ask for—everything except a mother.

"Time passed fast, but not to my father. I was seventeen when I graduated from high school and my father gave me a Ford, red and white. The first day after I finished school my father and I were sitting at the breakfast table, neither of us saying anything. Then dad cleared his throat and said, 'Son, I want to have a man-to-man talk with you.'

"After breakfast we walked out on the terrace and sat in a big swing that hung in the garden. Dad explained the plans he had made concerning my future.

" 'Calvin, as you know, your mother died during your birth and I prayed to God to spare your life. He did and I swore to myself and your mother that the world would know and respect you.' He went on to explain to me what he had planned for me ever since I was a child.

"I stood up and walked around the terrace with my head down. Then I said: 'Father, you should let me decide for myself what I want out of life.'

"I walked over to him and looked straight at him. He sat there, not saying a word. I continued: 'Do you understand? I don't want the world to know me; I just want to be let alone and to live my life. Is that asking too much? Ever since I can remember you've been making all the decisions for me, but that's all over now, it's all over.' I started to walk away, but I turned and added, 'I want to be happy without all the heartaches of trying to be what I'm not. I just want to love and be loved in return.'

" 'Love? Love is for weak men,' he said loudly. 'All I ask is for you to try to do one thing for me.' His eyes were full of tears, and in a way I felt sorry for him.

" 'Okay,' I said, 'what do you want me to do?'

"His plans were for me to go to college and take over his business. I wasn't surprised."

It was getting darker. Crouched there beside Calvin's foxhole I thought of many things while I listened to him talk. I thought, more or less professionally, that a good leader knows his men and what is in their minds. He knows what makes them the kind of soldiers they are. If he is any good at all, he knows also that war makes men want to talk, and because death is never very far away, he knows that sometimes they want to talk about themselves.

Here was a young soldier spilling out his life to me with no reserve at all. He told me about the girls in his life, and about how he had learned about sex, and about a tragedy in connection with that, and about his continuing failure to work things out with his father. The end of it all was his decision to enlist and volunteer for Vietnam duty. There was never a time when his father's money couldn't, he seemed to believe, have got him out of that foxhole from which he was talking to me, but he was a proud man, and he was doing something he had chosen for himself. And with all the advantages he could have had, I thought—money, and being white, and being on the right side of the tracks.

"There you have it, Sarge, a part of my life in a brown paper bag."

I hesitated. "Maybe what you're trying to do is find yourself out here, even in a foxhole."

"Well, yes. That, and leaving home—getting away from my father and the life I used to have."

Because I thought I understood what Calvin had been talking about, I was about to agree and go on my way when the sound came. We both heard it—the sound of a bugle. Armies don't use bugles much in Vietnam, and to hear the enemies' bugles is to know the sound of fury, a kind of foretaste of death. We both knew what the bugle meant. Out there were the Viet Cong—not one or two or a squad, but at least a full regiment. And then the firing started, mostly mortars, and the sound of the bugle was lost in the roar of the explosions.

"They're coming, they're coming!" Calvin was shouting against the roll of the explosions.

I shouted back, "Hold your position, man!"

It took only minutes to double back to the command post. Ben had the radio glued to his ear. "A surprise attack, Sarge. The whole battalion is under fire." He sounded frantic.

"Have you called the Old Man yet?"

"Yes, yes. He says hold your position and keep him posted."

Well, I thought, the platoon is well dug in. It would take all hell to move us. Listening, I could hear our jets beginning to strafe and bomb by the light of the moon. They came and they came.

Two hours later the enemy mortars had stopped, and there was an ominous silence. We braced ourselves for the final attack, sitting there in the darkness hour after hour. Finally it was morning and we were still waiting.

Ben looked at me. "What do you think, Sarge?"

"I don't know, Ben. It's daylight, and the Viet Cong aren't out there. Maybe only a few dead ones. That's all I can figure. In case company command calls, I'm going out to check our lines."

The first position I stopped at was Calvin's. It was quiet—no sign or sound of life. A few feet away from his foxhole was a dead Viet Cong.

"Calvin!" I called. "Calvin! Are you all right?"

There wasn't any answer. Then I saw him, a few feet away in the sand, face down.

I picked him up in my arms, but he was dead. There

was nothing more to say or think or feel. Killing and more killing.

Maybe the people in the world Calvin came from didn't even know he was in Vietnam, or why.

SEVEN

No Peace for
the Damned

Hours turned into days, days into months, and months into dreams. We marched on, through the jungles, over the rice paddies, and into a kind of lifelessness. Ambush patrols at night, platoon-sized patrols during the day, and one major operation after the other. . . .

"Sergeant Vance, the Old Man's on the radio and he wants to talk to you," Ben was yelling across the platoon from the command post.

I rushed over and answered. "Sergeant Vance, sir."

"Vance, we're moving out in one hour. I'll give you the order on the way out." His voice sounded sure and urgent.

By the time I had finished talking to the Old Man, Ben had all the squad leaders at the command post.

"Operation, men," I said bluntly. "We have to be ready to move in forty-five minutes."

"Where are we going, Sarge?" Kain asked.

"I don't know. The Old Man didn't say. I do know the 28th Infantry is out. Maybe we'll be going to help them."

"How long are we . . ." Sergeant West was normally curious.

"The Old Man's on the radio again, Sarge," Ben said.

"Sergeant Vance here, sir."

"Have your platoon on the road in front of the mess hall in five minutes."

"All right, sir. We're on our way." There was no doubt Ben was the best radio operator in the company. Already he had our gear ready to go.

"West, you lead out. You have one minute to move your men."

"Right," West said, and moved out.

"Kain, you bring up the rear. Let's move out, first platoon."

We moved out along the track we used every day going back and forth to the mess hall. When we reached the company area, all the other platoons were already lined up and ready to move. All the platoon leaders were seated in front of the company commander, as our platoon sergeants took charge of the platoons.

"I'm going to make this brief, men, because we don't have much time. The 28th Infantry has been hit north of Bau Bang. They don't need any help, but the Old Man thinks we may be able to catch the Viet Cong in a crossfire.

"Vance, you'll lead out. Keep to the right of Route 13. Cox, you follow the first platoon. Vance, you and Benson will put out flank security. Jackson, you cover the rear. The 28th is only two miles away so we should be in the south end of their position in no time."

"Will we have air cover, sir?" I asked.

"We'll have it on call. Now let's move."

We cleared the rubber plantation and my platoon broke out into the clearing and deployed along the road moving north. I walked to the front of the platoon, where Sergeant West was.

"I understand the 28th is doing a good job." West said.

"That's right. The word is they only lost one man."

"All of us squad leaders figured it was about time for us to try and find the Viet Cong. Those bastards have a simple and effective plan—'When the enemy advances, we withdraw; when he defends, we harass; when he's tired, we attack; and when he withdraws, we pursue.'"

"It may be simple, but it's very effective," I said.

"You better believe it," West answered.

When I looked back I saw the Old Man talking to Lieutenant Benson.

"What's the 28th supposed to be doing out here anyway, Sarge?" Ben asked.

"Stay off the road, Wheeler! You want to lose a leg or your life?" West suddenly yelled.

I waited till my ears stopped ringing. "Since our battalion is the reactionary force for the 28th, we gotta sit and wait until something happens, and then we move out in support or take over the mission. The 28th's operation was supposed to be one of those three-day missions: search and clear the area around Bau Bang north on Route 13."

Route 13 looked long and quiet as we moved, cautiously gaining on the 28th. We could hear small-arms fire in the distance and the jets were still dropping bombs. The company commander was up front with me as we moved up.

"Everything okay, Vance?"

"So far, sir. Hope it stays that way."

"So do I. Better head into the jungle line now. We should be close."

"Take a right, West, and watch the jungle line." West had his point man go to reconnaissance by fire before he moved into the jungle. Soon we were surrounded by the dark quiet jungle. We cut our way through and came out into another clearing, just south of the 28th. In the center of the clearing was the body of a GI. West quickly stopped the platoon. The Old Man was behind with the second platoon.

"There's a man out there, Vance, one of ours," said West.

"Put out security and set your guns here for cover. Kain, you take the left side. Roberts, take the right. Ben, get the Old Man on the radio."

"He's coming up, Sarge," Ben answered.

A few seconds later the company commander was with me, looking at the body. "Do you have security out?" he asked, casually.

"Yes sir, the area is covered."

"All right, just stand fast." He called the other platoons and had them deploy. Then he said: "Send two men out to check the body."

"Kain," I called. "Send two men out to check the body. Look out for traps."

The two men walked forward slowly, and we could hear them talking as they approached the body.

"Man, I hope this isn't an ambush," one of the said.

"If it is, we've had it."

The sun was hot and the air in the clearing was still. The rest of the company waited quietly.

Bob kneeled by the dead man. "Well, I'll just be damned—will you look at this!"

We could see Hilton shrink back. "He's not a GI. He's a damn Viet Cong with GI clothes on."

They both seemed to take deep breaths.

When the men made it back safely we all breathed easier. An hour later we linked up with the 28th. As we settled down for the night I ran into a buddy of mine named Lewis from the 28th and later, when we were all set up for the night, he came over and told me what had been happening.

The 28th had operated north of Bau Bang for about two days and found nothing, not even a trace. Yesterday they had pulled into this small clearing on the east side of old One-Three and made the perimeter in the center of the field. They had grazing fire up to six hundred meters, in all directions. At dawn they sent out three small ambush patrols; one set up near a trail five hundred meters north of Charley Company, and one traveled six hundred meters and set up on a small hill south of B Company. About two in the morning the patrol to the north reported they heard a large group of men double-timing down the trail they were set up on. It was a group of Viet Cong about the size of a company, they seemed tired from running. They stopped short of the ambush patrol where they had their Claymore mines in position. After the northern patrol called in, the patrol to the south reported they had spotted about three hundred civilians—women and children. There was also an old man dressed in white, like a priest, who was giving all the orders. According to the patrol leader, the women acted like they were being forced to do whatever had been planned for them. Some of them had old guns and ammunition; some of them had sticks.

The VC in the northern area started to advance and the patrol fired their Claymore mines. The blast caught the VC totally by surprise and the entire group panicked. The patrol then threw all their hand grenades, which added to the confusion.

Then the young lieutenant gave the order to pull back and re-enter the lines. The Viet Cong in Lewis' sector started firing in all directions, without control. The patrol to the east spotted another large group of Viet Cong and opened up on them, but the VC rushed them, and the patrol was so small it was run over. The squad leader, Sergeant Cabet, ordered his men to merge with the Viet Cong and act like part of them.

His men thought he was crazy, but by following his orders they made it back to their own lines. When the Viet Cong started firing on the eastern front, their mortars also started firing, which, the 28th later discovered, they weren't supposed to do until after they were in position. But the mortar rounds were going in the wrong direction, and they all fell on their own people. Most of the VC units in that area were cleaned out by their own fire.

As the patrol in the north was pulling back, the lieutenant spotted what he thought was the VC commanding officer. The lieutenant jumped into the road, fired, and threw a hand grenade, trying to kill this VC leader, and then he had to make it back alone. When he finally caught up with his men he found a soldier with a leg wound. The Cong had the rest of the patrol pinned down, but that gutsy lieutenant decided to go back to get the wounded man. One of the Negro sergeants volunteered to join him, and the two of them went back after the soldier. They found him, all right, but in trying to return they were cut off by a machine gun. The only way back was to knock out the gun. The lieutenant charged the machine gun and he got it—but they got him.

The battle went on until morning but by then the VC were so confused they were running all over the place and their leaders had little control. When the sun appeared, so did F-100 Saber jets. The 28th was running low on ammunition and needed resupply desperately, so the Old Man called for a resupply chopper and it was there in minutes. The fire on the ground was so intense that a fly would have been hit if it tried to fly. The commanding officer told the pilot they needed the ammunition, but that the chopper couldn't land under the firing conditions. The ignored the commanding officer and came in anyway, in spite of many VC hits. But when it took off a .50-caliber opened up on it from the line of the woods and it went down on Route 13.

I asked Lewis how many VC they'd gotten.

"We killed 240, and only lost three men. All the Viet Cong's plans were knocked to pieces because of some wise leadership. And again the Negro was a big factor in the entire situation, proving that he *is* capable."

"Why do you say that about the Negro?"

"Oh, I don't know, but it's true. The Negroes in the 28th are outstanding, but we're being used."

"I think the Negro casualty rate proves the point, but there's more to it than what people have been led to believe. Figures show that more Negroes have died in Vietnam than any other U.S. military personnel group, but most American officials deny there's any discrimination in the battle area assignments."

Lewis nodded agreement. "It's not a simple question of discrimination. All commanders use their best people, and often these men are Negroes. So, when something dangerous comes up, the best leaders are ordered to take charge. You can't refuse the duty. If a Negro failed to obey his orders he'd be punished, which would only be right. But now I'm beginning to feel this isn't the way it always is."

Lewis was right. "My company commander and I had it out a few days ago over something like this," I said.

Lewis said soberly, "In my unit, Vance, if a white soldier falls short, he's given a second chance, or removed from the front lines, which is what he wanted in the first place. I hear that the Viet Cong have a name for Negroes; they call us the 'black Americans'—the people with the tight hair and strong skin, the 'true Americans.'"

"I know, I've heard that, too. I'm sure you know there were times when the Viet Cong wouldn't kill or harm a Negro unless a unit was ambushed or attacked and the Negro was a part of it. There are places in Saigon where the Negroes can roam freely and stay out all hours of the night, and nothing ever happens to them. If a white man dared to travel anywhere alone, he'd be doomed."

"The Viet Cong say the Negro is braver than the white man, and they can't understand why. They say the 'black Americans' should not be in Vietnam, that he should be fighting a war back home for reasons similar to their own."

"All of my men are good, Vance, but my black boys are out of this world. My platoon leader was white and whenever he took a patrol out, you can bet his second in command was a Negro."

"A black man is known for his bravery throughout Vietnam. He knows what it takes. By now, so do a lot of the others. There can't be any doubt in our great white fathers' minds of the ability of the Negro to lead under combat conditions. Not any more."

The night was quiet. Evidently the Viet Cong had moved out to lick their wounds. Nothing happened that night, but the VC knew we were there and they would be back in one way or another.

The next morning we returned to the base camp, and when the men reached the platoon area they were very glad to get home to their foxholes. I took off my combat gear, found myself a corner of the command post, and relaxed, talking to Ben.

Then LeRoy and Davis came in.

"Have you heard?" Davis asked, moving close to me.

"Gilbert is dead," said LeRoy. There was sorrow and hurt in every line of his body.

"He's dead, Vance. He got it about thirty minutes ago

coming in off patrol." Davis' voice was shaking.

"My God!" I said in disbelief. "We just came in off operation—what was he doing on patrol so soon?"

"The Old Man wanted a listening post out; they think we may get hit tonight."

"God damn that Captain Berger," I protested in a rage. "Every time, every lousy time—it has to be a black soldier."

Quietly, Ben said: "I thought a great deal of Sergeant Gilbert."

LeRoy sat on the sandbags and picked away at the string that held the sand inside. Ben was looking at me.

"Gilbert was a great soldier," I said. "He wouldn't think of disobeying an order. But if he got sent out on patrol right after that last operation, he got a hell of a raw deal."

"I can't get over it," Davis said in a choked voice.

Then I got a call from the Old Man to report to him.

"Oh, man! We just got back, Sarge," Ben said, his voice trembling with rage. "I'm going to ask to get out of this platoon. Not because of you as a leader—you're the best—but because you're Negro. That's why we get all the shit around here."

I was bothered by Ben being so upset but there was no way of dealing with it then because I had to go to the Old Man's tent. I made a point of finding out later what they said after I left, though.

They had talked on about Ben's remark. He had meant it, and they agreed with him. Finally, however, he had said, "I didn't think I'd ever feel about a Negro like

I do Sergeant Vance. The only way I'll ever leave him is that I go home or I get it."

The company commander was worried; I could tell that by the way he moved his fingers in small circles. There was another officer with him when I reported.

"Sergeant Vance, Major Richards and I have a small problem we feel you can help us with."

I nodded. "Sir?"

As the Old Man talked, Major Richards took notes.

"The day you and your platoon were assigned to Charley Company on a road-clearing operation, a truck was blown up. One of the men in it was never found."

"That's why I'm here," the major said.

"We have to talk to everyone who was on the operation."

"Sir," I answered, "road-clearing operations are something we do all the time. It means going into Viet Cong territory—territory that's surely off limits to us. Every time we travel down thunder road, the 'bloody one-three,' we lose men. There's no way it can be stopped. The commanders know this, but it's not their lives," I said bitterly.

"There's no need for excitement, Vance," Captain Berger said.

"I'm not excited, sir."

"All I want to know is what went on that day," Major Richards said, standing up.

"Okay. Where should I begin?"

"Tell us everything, please."

So I told them. An hour after Captain Berger told me

I had the operation, we had moved down the road with the mission of clearing for the Vietnamese. We had been out just a little while when we heard an explosion, followed by the screaming of wounded men. When I arrived, I saw the remains of five men—a leg here, an arm there. One poor man had nothing from his waist down, part of his legs landed in front of me, and I was over a hundred meters away. Another of the men hurt was a good friend, a Negro I had met on the ship. I found him lying on the side of the road with both feet blown off at the ankles. He was a medic, and with two other medics working on him, he instructed them on how to cut off his feet.

The same day we had eight more men blown up in this area, yet the commanders still used the troops to clear the road of mines. My platoon called in to the company commander and told him both sides of the road were infested with land mines. His reply was: "Continue as ordered."

During the night the Viet Cong would plant land mines in the road and the only way we could find them was when someone walked on them or a truck rolled over them. That's how the men on the truck got it.

After I had finished, the major put his cap on, picked up his rifle, and said: "I think that will do for now, Sergeant Vance. However, you may have to tell your story again to the colonel."

"I have less than three months left in Vietnam, sir, so as long as he talks to me before my time is up . . ."

I smiled as the major walked past me and left the tent.

"Is that all, sir?" I asked the Old Man.

"No, Vance, we have a new officer in the company and I'm going to put him in your platoon."

"It's about time I got a platoon leader. Is he black?"

He answered: "One day, Vance, your mouth's going to get you into something you can't get out of."

"I can take care of myself, sir. I have for the last nine and a half months."

"No, he's not black. He's only a man."

My new platoon leader, Lieutenant Douglas, was waiting when I got back to my platoon. Before I reached the command post I could see him walking around in the area. He was tall and thin and had all of his combat gear on. He was very young, just like all of them are.

All the squad leaders had met Lieutenant Douglas. He was an ROTC officer and had spent most of his time at a basic-training center and knew very little about leading troops. We had a long talk. I told him all I could about the platoon and the ways of the enemy. He was very attentive, but he finally said he wasn't ready to take over and run the platoon. We decided I would continue to control the platoon until he felt he was ready to take over.

All went well for the first few weeks and then, about a month and a half later, he told me he was ready to take charge. His understanding of leadership was poor, but his ability to read a map was good. As far as I was concerned, all second lieutenants were the same.

Two days after Douglas arrived we were about to become one of the lead elements in one of the largest operations in the country up to that time—Operation "Double

Mastiff." We moved by air to the landing zone approximately forty miles from our base camp only a hour after we received the operation order. We made an assault landing and pushed forward as soon as we touched ground, advancing under light enemy sniper fire. That's the way it was for the rest of the day.

The next morning we were operating in an area infested by the enemy. We searched the jungle all day for what we thought was a Viet Cong battalion, but it turned out to be a Viet Cong regiment. This was a big operation and we were working with many other units in the area. At last we thought we had the Cong surrounded while another unit was to move in from the north for the kill. But the unit made only light contact when they were supposed to be heavily engaged, so again the enemy had evaded our forces.

All the same, the operation was clearly not over; there was some action yet to come, and again the Viet Cong would choose the time and place for the fight. Charlie is shrewd in many ways; he fights only when he wants to and when he feels sure of victory.

Alfa company had been in the field for four days and the company commander had just called to tell us the unit was staying in place for the night. So after another hard day in the jungle we set up our defense position in a dry rice paddy about 1,500 meters north of a small village whose people were believed to be friendly. After we received the order for the next day from the CO, Douglas and I passed it on to the men and then settled down for the night. Our company was to conduct clearing operations beyond the village for the rest of the battalion.

"So we're leading the company tomorrow, Lieutenant?" I asked.

"Yeah, we're leading," Douglas replied. "Do you think we'll make any contact?"

"It's hard to tell, but one thing's for sure—the enemy is no fool and he's not a poor fighter. Whenever we *do* engage him we'll have our hands full, and when it's over we'll know we've been in a hell of a fight."

"The Old Man told me you've been in a number of major battles and lots of assault landings and that you're more than qualified to teach me the art of the game."

"Yes, sir," I said. "I'll do my best." Douglas was always anxious to learn more about the methods of war, but time for teaching was short.

The next day started like all the others. We left right after first light, moving across the paddies looking for our evasive enemy. After an hour or so we came to a clearing opposite the village. The Old Man had said there was no need to clear it so we only paused for a few seconds and kept on pushing.

This clearing was a danger zone, and we should have gone around it, not through it, I thought as we deployed in an open formation and advanced across the area. Douglas was up front with the lead squad. I watched him walking proudly with the squad leader, and remembered how proud I'd been the first time I took command.

"I don't like this area," I said to Ben, my operator. "Don't like it at all."

"Think we should have cleared it first?" he asked

anxiously.

"Damn right."

We were all in the open now with no cover nearby and suddenly, like a quick rain storm, the crackling of rifle fire came from the village. Immediately the thumping of mortars and cries for the medic were all around us. There was only one way we could go, and that was forward.

We attacked aggressively, slowing up only for obstacles, and took and held the south end of the village. The men moved in and took up positions. I was checking my men when the company commander called about the casualty report. My area was okay, but I had to check the front elements of the platoon, so Ben and I went forward. The third squad was digging in and working very hard. They knew what it was like to be caught without a position if the VC attacked.

One man in the second squad was hit and Sergeant Kain was putting a splint on his leg.

"Everything okay, Kain?" I asked.

"Sure, we'll make it. I don't think his leg is too badly broken."

A few yards from Kain's position in the dark underbrush I spotted something that looked like a cave, with some old clothes lying aroud it.

"What the hell is that, Kain? Have you checked it out? Damn good way to get your ass shot off," I growled, knocking the safety off my rifle.

Ben and I moved toward it cautiously, when I saw two slanted eyes at the mouth of the cave. Without hesitating I fired. My shot missed by an inch, but within a second I was ready to fire again, and this time I was damn well not going to miss. Then I heard a baby start to cry. The cry shook me, and in the middle of firing I lowered my rifle and shot into the ground. A second later I saw that the eyes belonged to an old woman, and I had barely missed killing her and the child. I felt weak.

The old woman told us that after the VC had moved in the night before she had taken her children to the cave for safety, because she knew that when the Americans came the bombs always fell. I made my report to the CO and sent the old lady and her kids to the rear.

After we cleared the village, the company took a forty-minute break. My men were tired of the endless walking, killing, and burning. When we left the village there was no life there, only flames. Then we were on our way again, pushing through the jungle.

Over and over again we had been ignoring a basic law, which is never to walk on roads and trails, and now we were walking along a trail that was as good as posted "Viet Cong Alley." All along both sides were potential firing positions and firing lanes—a perfect place for an ambush. It reminded me, bitterly, of the battle of Michelin Plantation.

Leaving the trail, my lead squad penetrated the underbrush. Almost at once gunfire cracked, and everyone hit the dirt. One of our men never rose again. Again we took out our wounded and dead, we stayed there for about an hour doing nothing, just waiting for the Viet Cong to come find us. The company commander was lost, and, over the radio, apparently hated to admit it. Lieutenant Douglas decided to look for the sniper after he saw we were going to be stuck there for a while.

"I'm going to find that damn Viet Cong, Vance."

"Are you sure that's what you want to do, sir?" I asked, not wanting him to try it.

"I have to start sometime, and this is the time," he said, checking his ammunition.

He looked all around, trying to decide where the Viet Cong had fired from, and then he noticed a trench that looked like an operation post. He decided to search it.

"Kain, take a man and check your side."

"Just like that sir? Shouldn't we . . . ?"

"No," Douglas answered without hesitation. Then he took his men and went down the other side of the trench. After checking most of it, they came to a curve and as they made the turn, a sniper fired.

"Medic!" someone shouted almost in the next breath. "Get the medic over there, Sarge!"

"Doc! Doc! Up front," I called, heading toward the call for help. And then, over my shoulder, "Who is it, Gibbs?" I shouted.

"It's Kain, Sarge."

"No! Oh, no!"

"He tried to tell the lieutenant, Sarge, but you know how it's been lately. Kain's dead, Sarge."

"Get that lieutenant over here," I commanded.

Exhausted, Lieutenant Douglas stood looking down at Kain's body. "I should have listened to him; I should have." His voice was shaking.

"It's too damn late for that now," I said. "That's the problem with green lieutenants—they don't listen."

"Take it easy, Sarge," the medic said.

I shouldn't have answered back, but I did. "Kain was a damn good man—one of my best—before this lieutenant came along. The sniper who got Kain is long gone. We'll never get him now." The anger in me was almost like a wound.

Well, the commanding officer decided we had better move on. The sniper with the rifle went scot free, with a personal victory to his credit. Men we had respected and lived with died unnecessarily that day.

The operation ended without any major contact. Heading back to our base, we relaxed as the chopper rose high above the jungle and the sound of its blades filled our ears.

"Sergeant Vance, I understand why you said what you did out there when Kain got it," Douglas said. "I want you to know I don't blame you."

I looked into his eyes and said: "Thanks, sir. I had no right to talk to you in front of the men the way I did. The longer you're here, sir, the more you'll realize that the Viet Cong doesn't plan for any GI to leave Vietnam alive or unhurt, mentally or physically."

When the chopper landed at Lai Kae we were relieved; we felt we were home, even if it was only a home away from home.

After only three days in the base camp, there was another operation in the making for us. It seemed like someone thought we were the only infantry unit in the war.

Lieutenant Douglas and I were walking from the company commander's tent toward our command post on our fourth day in base camp. The air was warm, stale, and damp, as if it had been used too much.

"Captain Berger's a fine soldier, isn't he, Sergeant Vance?" Douglas asked, taking long strides.

I hesitated. "He used to be okay when we first got here, but a lot of things have happened to make me change my opinion of him."

"Like what?"

"Perhaps I see him a little differently from you since I'm a Negro. Now, Captain Berger is impartial between Negroes and Negroes, or between whites and whites, but a lot of us think he shows partiality between Negro and white."

"That's hard to believe, Vance."

"It's not if you've been with him for a while. Let me give you two examples, one about a white and one about a Negro. We had a big white sergeant with us who should have been thrown out of the Army a long time ago. He just about had his way in the company, and very little was done about it. When we first arrived in Vietnam, this man took off and went to Saigon. He was AWOL for six days, but nothing happened to him after he got back; the Old Man just talked to him and told him not to do it again. After we moved up to this area, this sergeant got drunk one evening, stole a machine gun, and shot up his platoon area. Again nothing happened to him. The last time he went AWOL to Saigon he didn't come back, and nobody knows where he is now. Berger is considered to be a good commander by all the white men, but the Negro troops can see through him. He's just like all other commanders—out for himself."

The cool night air settled around the command post. We fumbled around the dark inside for our bunks.

"That's one story, Vance, about a white. How does the story about the Negro differ?"

"We had a Corporal Palace assigned to the platoon," I said. "He was a good soldier, and it wasn't long before he proved himself to be a well-respected and capable leader. He proved himself in the face of the enemy, and the men in his platoon would have followed him to hell. But his platoon leader was white, and he had a one-track mind. One day the platoon sergeant and Corporal Palace had a few words and when the company commander heard about it he called Palace to the command post. All the Old Man could think of was the fact that Palace was a Negro. He didn't bother to remember the time the corporal saved the lives of six men in his company, or that he was one of our best leaders.

"No, the old man only cared about the fact that this Negro had given one of the white sergeants some back talk. Anyway, he finally got so mad he hit Palace, and Palace—figuring he had been hit first—came on with a left to the body and a right to the captain's head. The Old Man fell down and then the first sergeant came running in with his rifle and told Palace to stand fast or he'd kill him right there. Even though both the sergeant and the corporal were black, the sergeant had no mercy for him, or at least he didn't show it. That's the loyalty black Americans have for commanders, white or not."

"Is this Sergeant Day you're talking about?"

"Yes, sir."

"Well, I'm sure *you* know that one of our great white military leaders once said: 'I'd rather have ten Negro soldiers than fifteen white ones, even though I am a white man.' He felt the Negro was more loyal. He is, and will be, one of the best American leaders."

"Yes, and today the Negroes are proving just that. But how wrong can people be and how *long* can people be wrong?"

"I guess there're things I'll never learn, Sergeant. It's going to be hard for me to live up to the standards you've set here."

"You don't have to," I said. "Set your own. So after Sergeant Day ordered Palace to stand fast, he helped the captain to his feet. With blood running out of his mouth and blood all over his uniform, he stood in front of the black soldier, looking right into his eyes. His voice trembled as he spoke. 'You had better find you another home, nigger, because if you don't I'll kill your black ass, you understand?' Day was right there, but then he left and went back to the orderly room. As soon as the captain said 'understand?' Corporal Palace took one step back and landed another blow to the Old Man's head.

"This time the captain wasn't knocked down, and he kicked at Palace and missed. 'You black nigger you, I'll kill you for this. No one like you or your kind's going to push me around like this. I'll kill you. I'll kill all of you if I have to!'

"Some more men from the company gathered around, and Palace heard words from white men in Vietnam that he'd heard before back home in the States. 'That nigger hit the company commander—let's get him,' someone said, and they ganged up on Palace and knocked him down and kicked him.

"When the dust settled, what was left of the corporal no longer resembled a man. He was taken out of the company and put in jail a few days later. The captain received the Army Commendation Medal."

"Oh, come on, Sergeant, you must be kidding."

"No, I'm not, sir, I wish I was. The battalion commander knew what had happened in the company. That's why the corporal went to jail and our captain received the U.S. Army Commendation Medal."

Douglas and I talked for about two more hours, and then I went to sleep thinking of how it was going to be when I got home. I had been away to war so that men could walk freely. I was ready to go home to become a part of that other world.

EIGHT

Black and
Proud

A PAIR OF combat boots stood in the dust, alone. Behind them, stuck in the ground by its bayonet, was the rifle that had belonged to the soldier who had worn the combat boots. On the rifle was a blood-stained helmet. Our chapel was an old Army tent that stood behind the boots, the rifle, and the helmet. Today we were gathered to pay our last respects for a fallen comrade, a man whom we had loved. While the chaplain stood over the symbolic articles a warm breeze touched our faces.

"Sergeant LeRoy was our brother. Like the waters of the sea rushing with the morning tide, he came to this land so that others may live on. Sergeant LeRoy paid the supreme price, so I ask of you, God's children, let not this price be in vain."

Afterward there was silence. A still, penetrating silence. When the service ended, Davis and I walked away.

"Davis, if things keep going like they are, all the Negro soldiers will be dead. God knows I'm glad I'll be leaving this hell hole and going home in two days."

"I only wish I was going home in two days."

"I thought a lot of LeRoy; we used to have some good times together. I'll never forget the time when he and Gilbert came over to my house at Fort Devens. They were from Georgia, too, and we talked about old times at home and told jokes until two o'clock in the morning." I smiled as I remembered it.

Davis' voice trembled as we walked slower: "LeRoy told me about that. How far did Gilbert live from you at Devens?"

"Not too far. We could walk to each other's house."

Davis and I found a large tree near the mess hall and parked our tired bodies to wait for chow. The sad day finally closed its eyes. The cool evening breeze signaled the coming of another damp night.

"What are you going to do when you get home, Vance?" Davis asked.

"I don't know. I'll be so glad to get back I'm just going to play it by ear."

"LeRoy and I were going into business together, but now I don't know."

"LeRoy was pretty well off, wasn't he?"

"Yes, I think so. He told me about his business, and a lot about his wife, who died three years before he went into the Army. You know, to look at him you wouldn't think he was still in love with his wife."

"No, I never would have guessed." I thought of my own wife, and how alive she was, thank God.

Davis closed his eyes, opened and closed them again, and said: "I can still see the rifle sticking in the ground and the combat boots that don't belong to anyone any more."

"I was thinking about the same thing."

Then Davis talked some more about LeRoy, and, listening to him, I felt I knew LeRoy better than I had before his death. He had, I realized, enlisted in the Army and volunteered for Vietnam partly because he could not bear to break with the memory of his dead wife or live with being untrue to her memory. He couldn't bring himself to marry again, though there was nothing to prevent him from doing so. Like a lot of lonely people, he had to be his own judge, and he finally gave himself a sentence which had now turned out to be a death sentence.

How much more fortunate, I am, I kept thinking to myself, than my friend. I'm going home, my wife is alive and waiting for me, and I've survived. I've survived this war, at least, and maybe I'll survive whatever else is ahead once I'm back home. I don't have to face the emptiness that LeRoy couldn't live with. At the end of Davis' story I found I didn't know what I thought, really, except that not all the wars are between people. Some are inside a man himself, and they are the loneliest.

I left Davis under the tree because I decided I didn't want chow after all. As I walked away, deep in thought, the small trail in front of me unrolled and I could read some of what it had to say. Along this trail had walked a lot of men who came to serve a cause, LeRoy among them. The dust of this pathway would not be stirred again by their feet. When I got to my bunk I fell on it, troubled and tired, and yet so excited about going home I couldn't sleep.

I lived through the agony of waiting, and the day finally arrived when I waved goodbye to my battle friends and left Vietnam. This time it was plane passage all the way. As we took off, I felt like I was coming out of hot hell and into the cool air of the normal world again.

"Man! Isn't it good to be going home?" a voice behind me said.

I looked around. "You speaking to me?"

"Yes, I am; I'm alone back here, and I thought I'd come up and talk to you."

"Please do," I replied.

The man was an old Negro sergeant major with hair that was white around the edges and a voice that was slow and calm.

"What unit were you with, Sergeant?" he asked, settling into the seat next to mine. He looked at my chest. "Sergeant Vance."

"First Division. And you?"

"The 25th. I had some friends with the First. Where you from in the States?"

"I was born in Georgia, but I haven't lived there for over six years."

"My home is Rhode Island. Born there, and I guess I'll die there."

"I'll be so glad to get to Georgia I won't know what to do."

"I know just what you mean. Me, I'll be glad to get back myself, not just for the sake of being in the States, but to have a chance to work for the Negro cause. I've fought in Vietnam, and now I'm going to demand what's due me."

I looked at him more closely. He didn't look like a hothead, and he was sure no kid.

"What's your name?" I asked.

"Ray. Just call me Ray."

"Ray," I told him, "I'm with you. I'm going to have my rights, too. I've seen too many men die, and I've lost too many men in that hell hole for me to go back and be some kind of an inferior citizen. I'm coming home from Vietnam not quite the same as I left. I've got a hell of a lot more pride and perspective. I'll be walking with my shoulders back and my chest out."

Ray nodded his grizzled head. "I know the problems you must have had as a platoon sergeant. I was a battalion sergeant major myself. Working with those officers wasn't the easiest part, even if some of them were good men. My battalion commander was white, and one day we were talking over a beer. All of a sudden he looked at me and said, 'You're a Negro, and you're over here fighting in a funny kind of war. How do you feel about all that, and your people's situation back home?'

"I looked at those silver leaves he had on before I answered. 'Sir, my hair is black and it grows in tight curls; my nose is large; my lips are thick; my voice is heavy and deep; my skin is black. Sir, my hair is curly because for so many years I been so flustered with the hate of my people that it couldn't grow straight; it curled from lack of security. My nose is large because day after day I had to follow behind the white man and I was so busy doing that I couldn't breath the fresh air of freedom. My features are a part of my identity; they're mine until I die. But now I can stand as a man. Now I can stand alone, as a free man, and never be ruled or conquered again. I hope that answers your question, sir.'

"The commander didn't get angry; he smiled and said that the question I'd get asked was do all Negroes feel that way, and he reminded me I was only one Negro, only one individual.

"I was surprised, but I answered that even though I was only one man, deep down inside all Negroes feel this way. Those who don't get to Vietnam might never understand that this land of the little dragon is our turning point, our stand, our time of truth, but they'll have to find their own moment of truth and make their stand in the streets of American cities."

Sergeant Ray pulled off his shoes. "How many kids do you have, Vance?" he asked, adjusting his headrest.

"One. A son. What about you?"

"Four boys."

"You know, it's a funny question, maybe, but while you were in Vietnam, did you find yourself thinking about your wife more than you ever have?"

"You better believe it." Sergeant Ray's voice sounded both amused and bitter.

"Me too. It sounds crazy, but I'm glad I wasn't single. My wife and my family were my dream. Sure, I remembered all the bad times we had, too, but I thought about ways to correct them when I got home. We'd been married for four years when I left, but we had only been together off and on for about a year and a half. I always seemed to be on the move, going to another base or another country, always having to leave my family behind."

Ray grunted. "What the hell can you do when your

number comes out of that computer in Washington? You move, man—family or no family. *And* you hate it. There are no really dedicated men in the service today. Being dedicated to the Army means that your family and loved ones are second. Only fools can feel that way."

"You're right. That's why you see so many men getting out of the service these days."

Ray nodded again, and then after a pause he said, in a different tone of voice, "I been thinking about what I'm gonna say when I get back with the family."

"Say?" I was puzzled.

"Yeah. About the war and the Army and what kind of future they figure to have—the kids, I mean—and all the rest of the business." He gave me an amused smile. "You're pretty good with words. I suppose you got it all figured out?"

I had to laugh. "You catch on fast, Ray," I said. "I've been trying to write something for Gary—that's my son. It's down on paper, but it's in my barracks bag. I remember it pretty well, though."

"Shoot," said Sergeant Ray. "Maybe it'll be a help."

"Well," I said, "I started off by telling Gary that I served my time in Vietnam just like many other American soldiers, and just like a lot more are going to have to do before the war is over. I told him I served with a lot of pride, and that I thought I had learned a lot, too, about myself, about other men, and about the Army."

Ray listened patiently and with interest as I rambled on, and several times he nodded in emphatic agreement. The first time was when I said that what was going on in Vietnam was really a war, and a full-scale one at that, not any mere "conflict."

A second nod accompanied my statement that most Americans go to Vietnam because they've been ordered to go, and for no other reason. They go and they do their job, maybe not willingly, but they do their job as ordered. But me? I went to Vietnam for another reason. Oh sure, I was ordered to go and I served because I was ordered to, but I also served with a special kind of pride that gave me standards higher than those of most of the men. I felt that, being a black man, I had to push for excellence. I had to stand out more. I had to show people that here was one individual black who was going to make Vietnam a place to be remembered as a first trial of leadership by black Americans.

I was successful, and in the process I found that some of my initial motivations were selfish. I learned that in a war a man is a man, and when you look across the foxhole into another man's face you see a friend—someone you can rely on, and you don't worry about the color of that face.

I went to Vietnam to prove something. I didn't necessarily go to play a direct role in aiding the South Vietnamese, even though that was the official reason. Inside myself I had my own reasons. During my time there I found that my real aim was to help those poor, struggling people, even though back home my own people were also struggling and trying to achieve a decent life.

The old sergeant nodded again when I said that I felt the United States forces ought to stick it out in Vietnam.

If we pulled out now, all the men who had died for that nation and our nation would have died in vain. Vietnam was responsible for washing away some of my prejudiced thoughts and for opening my eyes to more problems in this world than my own problems.

In Vietnam I often looked at the poor, deprived children and thought of my own people back home and how little they had. But what mattered in Vietnam was that I was helping the people right *there*, even though I often prayed that other people could look at my people and other minority groups and feel this same compassion.

Vietnam was a proving ground for me. Vietnam is a proving ground for many soldiers, especially black soldiers. We all have one common desire—to carry our load and bear our share of the responsibility so that when the war is over and we have finally all returned home the people in the United States will recognize that Negroes carried their responsibilities and shed their share of the blood in Vietnam.

My time is over in Vietnam. I'm fortunate. I'm one of those who can walk away from it and remember the hardships and the cries, and who can still say, "Thank God I'm alive." I'm one of those who can truthfully say that I saw a nation in desperate need, and I tried to help. That nation took my hand and thanked me for my efforts.

Now that it's all over I can honestly say I'm glad I had a chance to go, a chance to go and play my part as a black American. I'm glad to say that I know for a fact that the Negro soldiers are outstanding, and that we are truly helping the South Vietnamese.

People say, "Pull out of Vietnam. We have no right to be there." But did the French have a right to ship arms to America during their struggle against the British? Does a nation need a reason to help another struggling nation that is being overpowered by a government that it has no desire to be ruled by? Vietnam has stimulated a lot of questions, some that can be answered and some that can never be. I'm proud to be part of a nation that has armed forces that fight to free others from bondage, and proud to be part of this courageous fighting force. But I'll be even more proud when this same courage is used to deal with the evils in my own country and to help gain the freedom of my people.

"So," I said, turning to Sergeant Ray, "that's about the message."

"I read it," he said. "I read it loud and clear. I hope little Gary does too."

"So do I."

Ray was silent for a whole; it was evident, though, that something was still bothering him. "Vance," he asked finally, "has your wife said anything in her letters about receiving crank telephone calls while you've been away?"

"No, thank God. Why do you ask?"

"My wife wrote me about this call she got. Some man was trying to get her to tell me to stay in Vietnam because I'm a Negro. He said Vietnam is the place for all blacks. Only a madman would say anything like that."

I had to swallow before I could answer. "No madman. The bastard had to be white," I said finally. "We've paid with our blood for the right to come home, and we're not going to settle for anything less than total freedom when we get there. We don't want anything we haven't earned, but we want what we have earned."

"Well, in a round-about way that's what my wife said."

Sergeant Ray and I got to know each other well before the flight was over. We talked all the way back, for hours and hours.

Then we heard: "Fasten your seat belts please, and observe the No Smoking signs. We will be landing at Travis Air Force Base in fifteen minutes. We hope you have enjoyed your flight."

And then the wheels were touching the ground. I was home in the good old U.S.A.

I caught the next thing smoking out of the field and on to Georgia. Four hours later I was at the Atlanta airport. There was a good-sized crowd there, mostly white. I was wearing my Army green uniform, and it couldn't have been hard to guess where I was coming from, but the hating, familiarly rejecting faces hadn't changed. Ribbons, uniform, and all, I was still *not*. I hadn't expected any miracle of acceptance, but still those white faces were no welcome-home committee. I cleared the crowd around the arrival gate. Far in the background, beautiful, waiting for me, was Barbara. Suddenly I was running toward her, and then our arms were around each other.

A lot has been said in these pages about what the black man has accomplished in Vietnam, and the black man has made a good name for himself there. And although a lot has been accomplished in this country, a lot more still has to be done. Those young black men who have not served in Vietnam will have to find their own moment of truth and, maybe, as Sergeant Ray said, make their stand in the streets. Maybe the Army experience is not the tougher of the two, but I find it hard to answer the people who ask me if I think military service is a step ahead for a Negro.

In some ways, yes. The Army can prove valuable to the Negro career soldier in that it can lead to a more prestigious life than he can achieve as a civilian in some prejudiced areas of the United States. But in most cases, any black man who is successful in the military will more than likely be successful in civilian life also.

Let no one be misled. In spite of integration, there is prejudice in the armed forces. As long as people have different personalities, there will always be someone prejudiced against somebody else. In the service, the Negro is not confronted as directly with the problems of bias and prejudice as he is in civilian life, but he is confronted with a more conservative, quiet kind of prejudice, if that is the appropriate description.

When a Negro professional soldier sets out to win a promotion, more pay, or more responsibility, he isn't told that he can't apply for the promotion. Instead, he often gets word that his personnel papers simply didn't get affirmative action, and that's the end of that. What if, as sometimes happens, the man persists and continues to trace his personnel-action papers? He'll probably be harassed by subordinate leaders within his own unit, whatever that unit may be, because these little subdivisions are almost always run privately, even though the Table of Organization shows them as part of a larger headquarters.

This kind of thing doesn't happen frequently, but it *does* happen. Yet, overall, I'd say that the Negro soldier get about as fair a shake as any other soldier in the Army.

Some of my Negro friends who have heard me say I thought the Army was essentially fair to Negro soldiers and offers a good road to a self-respecting career are skeptical. "Why should there be a more walk-tall life in the armed forces than in civilian life?" they demand. I'm not sure of the answer, partly because practically my whole adult life has been spent in the Army, but perhaps the uniform itself has something to do with it.

Most men who wear the uniform of their country learn to wear it with pride. It becomes a part of one's image of himself. When he's noticed on the street by civilians, they see an emblem of their country in that uniform, and the man wearing it is seen primarily for what he is, a soldier, and less directly as being either white or black.

The Negro soldiers with whom I have served were proud to wear their uniforms, and they walked taller because of that pride. But there is more to the question than the uniform itself. Certainly another element is the responsibility, which can be earned faster and at a higher level in the Army than in any other way of life I know. Responsibility is a duty, but it is also a trust. There isn't any man, black or white, who isn't proud to be trusted.

Some weeks ago I was attempting to convey to a white friend of mine a part of what I've tried to say in these final pages. My friend, who is not a soldier or a veteran, was not convinced.

"It seems to have come out that way for you," he observed. "You're certainly proud of that uniform and of the trust, but you may be an exception."

"I don't think I am."

"I'd like to believe you." He paused. "It's a little puzzling. You and your black companions seem to want the full democratic treatment in this country, and yet you seem to have got more democratic justice out of the Army. I certainly don't think of the Army as a democratic institution."

"Believe me, the Army doesn't either. But the Army puts itself ahead of everything else, including the color of a man's skin or the nature of his faith."

My friend still didn't seem convinced.

So I told him about a little daydream of mine that I hoped would help explain my feelings. In this daydream I'm talking to a bunch of privates I've just taken through eight weeks of basic training. I'm giving them a kind of graduation speech. My uniform is starched to a T. My brass is shining and reflecting the sun. My spit-shined boots are highly glossed. My appearance is almost perfect and there is a shadow behind me. All of my privates are sitting in front of me waiting quietly for me to summarize their situation. I stand with my hands behind me. I'm comfortable and relaxed. I speak.

"All of you men look different today. I can remember you when you first came to the Army, fresh off the streets and farms of our nation. You came as civilians with papers stating that you were soldiers. Together, in the barracks and on the hillsides of this training area, we found ourselves, and those papers are true, now. We have become people that we didn't know it was in us to become. We are now United States soldiers.

"So, I want to talk to you on a subject all of you are going to be confronted with throughout your military career, whether it be two years, three years, or twenty years. That subject is togetherness.

"Now, I'm sure you men all realize that the United States Army is not a democratic institution. In understanding that, you must also know that you're going to be dealing with people from different races, different religions, and of completely different personalities. During your eight weeks of training you had to sleep together, eat together, play together, and train together, but where some of you are going, you're going to have to eat together, fight together, and die together. This is the reality. There are no secrets. There are no hidden motives behind the reactions of the United States Army.

"I want to say something about that thing of togetherness once you get to the Republic of Vietnam. While you're there, you men are going to have to trust each other and believe in each other's ability to see a job through. You're going to have to lean on each other whether the man you lean on is black, white, or red.

"All of you were taught various thing about one another in the past. Your cultural standards are different, and so are your backgrounds. But in Vietnam you will look at a man and you will not judge that man by what you see on the surface. You will judge him by what he does. You will judge him by his character and you will judge him according to the way he functions.

"Gentlemen, your task hereafter is not going to be easy. Your road is not going to be smooth, and your path is not going to be clear. But all of you have received proper training, and it works. It will follow you until the very last day. Now it's up to you. It's up to you to utilize the physical and mental training you have received, including the information you are receiving here and now.

"You must have learned that no one—no one type of person—is perfect. You're going to have to give and take. Yield and seek. In doing this you'll find that your mind is broadening to the conditions of our country and of the world."